W9-BVF-748

The Book of
Zen

The Book of

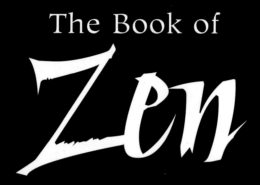

Zen

Eric Chaline

BARRON'S

A QUARTO BOOK

First edition for the United States,
its territories and dependencies,
and Canada published in 2003 by
Barron's Educational Series, Inc.

All inquiries should be addressed to:
Barron's Educational Series, Inc.
250 Wireless Boulevard
Hauppauge, New York 11788
http://www.barronseduc.com

Copyright © 2003 Quarto Inc.

All rights reserved. No part of this book may
be reproduced in any form, by photostat,
microfilm, xerography, or any other means, or
incorporated into any information retrieval
system, electronic or mechanical, without the
written permission of the copyright owner.

International Standard Book No.
0–7641–5598–9

Library of Congress Catalog Card No.
2002106706

QUAR.TBZ

Conceived, designed, and produced by
Quarto Publishing plc
The Old Brewery
6 Blundell Street
London N7 9BH

Project Editor: Kate Tuckett
Art Editor: Karla Jennings
Assistant Art Director: Penny Cobb
Designer: Caroline Grimshaw
Copy editor: Jean Coppendale
Picture Research: Image Select International
Proofreader: Anna Amari-Parker
Indexer: Pamela Ellis

Art Director: Moira Clinch
Publisher: Piers Spence

Manufactured by
Universal Graphics Pte Limited, Singapore
Printed by
Midas Printing International Limited, China

9 8 7 6 5 4 3 2 1

Contents

INTRODUCTION

"What is the sound of one hand clapping?" This short question, or koan, *sums up much of the philosophy of Zen Buddhism. What is the educated, twenty-first century man or woman to make of this seemingly irrational nonsense?*

Many claim that Zen is nothing more than an elaborate trick that has been played on a gullible public for almost 1,400 years; others believe that it's the single most important shift in human consciousness.

Although Zen is surrounded by the paraphernalia of religion, it is clearly not a religion in the same way as Judaism or Christianity. Christians believe that if they obey the Church's Commandments, they will, in some future existence, be rewarded or punished for their actions in this life. To this essentially passive view of salvation, we must compare the active search for *satori*—liberation or enlightenment—that is at the center of Zen. Satori is not a deferred reward; it is a state to be experienced here and now. Nor is satori the final goal of Zen because, in reality, it represents the beginning of Zen life.

No book on Zen philosophy can hope to give a map to enlightenment. Each of us has our personal road to that goal. However, it can relate the experiences of those who have gone before and can act as a guide for our steps.

With the above limitation in mind, I have attempted to present a comprehensive

This Amitabha Buddha (or Buddha of Infinite Life) is presented in traditional form: both hands in a contemplative gesture.

Although Zen monks live under a strictly ascetic regimen, their surroundings are often ornate and highly decorative.

background to Zen Buddhism—tracing its origins in the teachings of the historical Buddha, Siddharta Gautama (The Root of the Flower), and its journey from India to China and Korea (The Stem of the Flower), before it finally reached Japan (The Petals of the Flower). In doing so, I have presented the main schools of Zen and introduced the leading personalities sustaining them. After an explanation of Zen principles and practice (Plucking the Flower and The Flower Blooms), I look at how Zen has influenced Japanese and Western culture—an interaction that is increasingly influential in many fields (The Ways of the Flower).

CHAPTER ONE

THE ROOT OF THE FLOWER

THE
ROOT OF THE
FLOWER

Along with Christianity and Islam, Buddhism is often described as one of the world's great monotheistic faiths. However, to equate Christianity, with its concepts of the immortal soul and a single omnipotent godhead, with Buddhism, which believes in neither; and correspondingly Jesus Christ, the self-proclaimed "Son of God," with the historical Buddha, Siddharta Gautama, would be to misunderstand Buddhism completely.

Buddhism emerged from the rich and varied polytheistic Hindu tradition, with its dizzying pantheon of gods and goddesses. In its early history, Buddhism was seen as an unorthodox or heretical school of Hinduism and in later times, an attempt was made to reconcile the two faiths by making the Buddha an incarnation of the Hindu god, Vishnu. On its long journey eastward, Buddhism was also much influenced by other polytheistic or animistic faiths, such as Bon in Tibet, Taoism in China, and Shinto in Japan.

In the centuries following the death of the historical Buddha (486 B.C.E.), Buddhism was adopted as the official religion of several powerful Indian states. Its greatest royal advocate was the Emperor Ashoka (third century B.C.E.), who ruled over the first Indian empire. After having converted to Buddhism, Ashoka renounced his policy of conquest by war, and replaced it with a policy of non-violent "Conquest by Righteousness."

Indian missionaries took Buddhism south to the island kingdom of Sri Lanka and to Southeast Asia, an area already within the Indian sphere of cultural influence. The Silk Route, which linked China to Europe via Central Asia, was also a conduit for Indian Buddhist thought toward the East

The Buddhist world extends north from India into Central Asia, and eastward to encompass all of East as well as Southeast Asia.

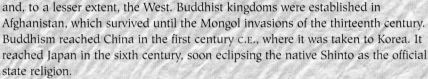

and, to a lesser extent, the West. Buddhist kingdoms were established in Afghanistan, which survived until the Mongol invasions of the thirteenth century. Buddhism reached China in the first century C.E., where it was taken to Korea. It reached Japan in the sixth century, soon eclipsing the native Shinto as the official state religion.

Buddhism declined in India and finally disappeared under the twin blows of the Islamic invasion of northern India in the tenth century C.E., and a Hindu revival in southern India. In the modern Indian subcontinent, Buddhism survives in the Himalayan kingdoms of Nepal, Bhutan, and Sikkhim, and on the island of Sri Lanka. In Southeast and East Asia, Buddhism has had a long and, until recently, uninterrupted history, and continues to thrive in Thailand and Japan.

THE TRUTHFINDER

The founder of Buddhism, Siddharta Gautama, was born a prince but lived as a pauper in ancient India.

Although the faith which the historical Buddha, Siddharta Gautama (566–486 B.C.E.), taught has been carried far beyond his homeland, his own ministry never took him more than a few hundred miles from his birthplace at Lumbini, near the borders of modern-day India and Nepal.

Over the centuries, many legends have grown around the life of the Buddha. In Zen Buddhism, in particular, the many fantastic tales and miracles ascribed to the Buddha are rejected: the Buddha is seen as an entirely human teacher who was

The canonical texts tell that Queen Maya gave birth while standing in a garden. When the Buddha emerged, he is said to have immediately taken seven steps. These are symbolized here by seven lotus flowers.

In early Buddhism, the Buddha was represented only in symbolic form, but from around the first century B.C.E., it became desirable to create images for oneself and one's descendants, and the Buddha's image became central to art, iconography, and ritual.

gifted with a unique insight into the nature of reality.

The most commonly accepted tradition has it that Siddharta Gautama was the son of Suddhodana, one of the *rajas*, or elected rulers, of the Shakya warrior clan. A privileged child, he was shielded from human misery until, as a young man, he saw, in turn, an elderly man, a sick man, and a corpse. Realizing that humanity's lot was to suffer old age, disease, and death, he determined to devote his life to freeing humankind from the cycle of death and rebirth, so that they could all achieve enlightenment—satori or nirvana.

Abandoning wealth, status, and family, he first studied the *Vedas*, the holy texts of Hinduism, under the foremost scholars of the day. After learning all they knew, he left them, realizing that salvation could not be reached through the intellect alone. He became a yogi ascetic and mortified his body. But after six years of privations that almost killed him, he understood that this asceticism would not bring him the answers he sought.

Shunned by his former disciples, close to despair, he decided to make one last attempt to gain enlightenment. For three days and nights, he meditated under a *bodhi* tree, where, on the dawning of the final night, he finally achieved enlightenment at the age of 35. After a lifetime of preaching he died at Kushinagara, now in the Indian state of Uttar Pradesh.

TURNING THE
WHEEL OF THE LAW

The Buddha's most profound teachings are encapsulated in the simplest of statements: the Four Noble Truths and the Eightfold Noble Path. Their study and practice over the past two-and-a-half millennia have given rise to some of the world's most complex philosophical systems and ritual practices.

Although he himself had attained enlightenment, the historical Buddha decided to remain in the world and devote his life to teaching. In his first sermon in Varanasi, in northern India, he expounded the doctrine of the Four Noble Truths:

> Life is suffering.
> Suffering is caused by selfish craving.
> Selfish craving can be overcome.
> Follow the Eightfold Noble Path.

This short statement encapsulates the Buddhist philosophy. The world is transient and, although some things within it are pleasurable, they, too, must pass. Transience leads to suffering. Our suffering, therefore, is not only caused externally by agents such as disease, famine, and death, but also internally by our own slavish pursuit of material and physical happiness. Our belief that we have an immutable ego or personality—a soul—keeps us prisoners of our desires which, when disappointed, leads to pain and sorrow. To overcome these illusions, the Buddha taught his disciples to follow the Eightfold Noble Path:

The Wheel of Buddhist Law symbolizes the endless cycle of birth and re-birth. The eight spokes represent the Eightfold Noble Path.

Correct thought
Correct action
Correct effort
Correct speech
Correct livelihood
Correct attention
Correct concentration
Correct understanding.

The Eightfold Noble Path is also known as the Middle Way, because it rejects all extremes of behavior. The Path embodies both moral injunctions, such as correct speech (not telling lies or spreading gossip), and correct livelihood (not pursuing an occupation that will do harm to other living beings). It also includes teachings on how to pursue enlightenment through study and meditation.

Finally, the Buddha enjoined his disciples to find comfort in the Three Refuges or the Three Jewels:

The concept of a symbolic path is central to Buddhist thought. The path shown above winds up the hill to a Buddha in a meditative position of perfect tranquility.

The Buddha;
The *Dharma*, the teachings of the Buddha;
The *Sangha*, the community of believers.

In early Buddhism, it was thought that only ordained monks and nuns of the Sangha could achieve enlightenment, but in subsequent interpretations of Buddhism, including Zen, lay men and women are also believed to be able to achieve enlightenment while still in the temporal world.

THE GREAT AND SMALL
COMPASSIONS

In modern Buddhism, liberation from karma and the cycle of death and rebirth can be achieved by following one of two traditions or "vehicles."

Buddhism is divided into two major traditions, or "vehicles," which offer different interpretations of what a person chooses to do once enlightenment has been attained. These are called the Greater (*Mahayana*) and Lesser (*Hinayana*) vehicles. The two were established by followers of the ultimately more successful Mahayana tradition. A form of Hinayana Buddhism survives in Sri Lanka and in Southeast Asia, where it is referred to as Theravada Buddhism (Teaching of the Ancients) or Pali Buddhism (resting on canonical texts written in the Pali language). It claims to be the form of Buddhism practiced by the Buddha himself.

Sometime during the second century of the Common Era, the Indian philosopher Nagarjuna proposed the concept of emptiness (*sunyata*), which led to the emergence of the Mahayana tradition. He argued against the Hinayana school, which held that, although all phenomena are empty because of their impermanence, they possess a true "self-nature." Nagarjuna maintained that the true nature of reality is to be totally devoid of permanent self. Nagarjuna's place in Mahayana Buddhism is so great that he is recognized as a second Buddha.

While the followers of Hinayana are said to pursue only their own liberation, stopping when they themselves are enlightened, the followers of Mahayana work to become *bodhisattvas* (enlightened beings) whose aim is the liberation of all sentient beings. Hence other names for the traditions are the "greater" and "lesser" compassions. The Mahayana tradition is predominant in Tibet, Mongolia, China, Vietnam, Korea, and Japan. Hence, both Chinese Ch'an and Japanese Zen Buddhism are part of the Greater vehicle.

Elaborate temples of the Mahayana tradition, such as this one in China, are also found in Tibet, Mongolia, Vietnam, Korea, and Japan.

SCATTERING TO THE
FOUR WINDS

Indian Buddhist missionaries traveled along the Silk Road to bring their faith to Central Asia, and then to China and Japan.

Like the early Christian Church after the death of its prophet, Jesus Christ, the Buddhist *sangha,* or community of believers, was prone to schism and dispute after the passing into *paranirvana* (final nirvana) of the historical Buddha, Siddharta Gautama. Scholars have identified dozens of competing schools within the Hinayana tradition, of which the Theravada school is the sole survivor in the modern world. These divisions were created by different interpretations of the Three Jewels or Refuges (the Buddha, the Dharma, and the Sangha). They were often influenced by the interventions of Buddhist rulers for their own advantage, just as the Roman emperors of Constantinople influenced the councils of the early

Tibetan Buddhists, despite decades of persecution, still practice a unique form of Buddhist ritual.

Arriving in Japan from China and Korea in the sixth century, Buddhism fused with and subsequently absorbed many defining elements of the indigenous Shinto religion.

Christian Church. These differences, however, did not lead to bloodshed or war, but to this day, the many schools of Buddhism claim that they alone have the correct interpretation of the Dharma and are the rightful recipients of the Dharma-succession from the historical Buddha.

The Theravada Buddhists of Sri Lanka and Southeast Asia can claim, with some justification, to be the closest to the original teaching of the historical Buddha since they reject the many additions made by later Mahayana philosophers. Within the Mahayana tradition itself, there are many competing schools. The Tibetan-Mongol Vajrayana school is based on its own sacred esoteric cannon, the *Tantras*. The Tibetan claim to superiority rests on the complexity of its philosophical system and elaborate rituals, which have become better known in the West since the expulsion of the Dalai Lama from Tibet by the Chinese in 1959. To make matters even more complex, Tibetan Buddhism is divided into four major schools.

The Chinese, Korean, and Japanese schools form the second major stream of Mahayana Buddhism. As we shall see, these three countries have incredibly rich and active Buddhist traditions. In each case, Buddhism came into contact with a vibrant local religion. The main schools of Chinese Buddhism included Ch'an, Tientai, and Pure Land, which would eventually be transplanted to Japan as Zen, Tendai, and Jodo. Japan, although it was the last of the great East Asian cultures to receive Buddhism, sometimes has claimed that its own schools are superior. The Japanese use the following image to justify their claim: if India is the root of Buddhism and China is its stem, Japan is then the flower, the culmination of a long process of development that has led from the historical Buddha to Zen.

CHAPTER TWO

THE STEM OF THE FLOWER

THE STEM OF THE FLOWER

Although it was destined to fail, Chinese Buddhism established the Mahayana tradition in both Korea and Japan.

In its journey through Asia, Buddhism first settled in China and Korea, where it developed deep roots and was influenced by native philosophies and religions. Buddhism of the schools of the Hinayana tradition reached China during the Han dynasty (206 B.C.E.–221 C.E.), when it was adopted as the official state religion. It made little headway among the general population, however, until the unsettled Northern and Southern dynasties period (219–580 C.E.).

Missionaries from India brought the teachings of the Mahayana tradition to China, and Chinese monks made the perilous journey West to study in India.

The Golden Age of Chinese Buddhism was during the T'ang dynasty (618–906 C.E.). Over the centuries, after its arrival in China, Buddhism had been transformed by Taoism and Confucianism, and had become integrated into Chinese culture. The two most popular forms of Buddhism during the T'ang period were the Pure Land and Ch'an schools. The Pure Land school taught a simple faith: no matter how depraved humans are, they can obtain liberation through belief in the Buddha. After the Muslim conquest of northern India, Chinese Buddhism became isolated from its Western origins. Despite flourishing in the Sung dynasty, Buddhism was subject to some persecution and began a slow and inexorable decline. It was swept away with all other religions by the Communist Revolution of 1949.

Chinese Mahayana Buddhism was introduced to the Korean peninsula during the Three Kingdoms period

In China, Indian Buddhas and bodhisattvas acquired Chinese names and appearances.

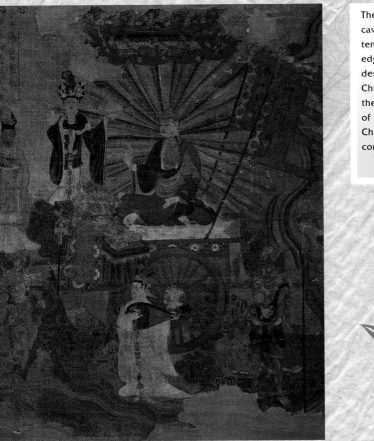

The Dunhuang cave art, from cave temples at the edge of the Gobi desert in northwest China, represents the work of some of the earliest Chinese Buddhist communities.

(c. 350–668 C.E.). Buddhism remained the dominant religion until the fourteenth century, when the rulers of the Neo-Confucianist Yi dynasty (1392–1901 C.E.) challenged its supremacy, fearing the power of the Buddhist establishment. Many monasteries and temples were closed and rival schools were forced to merge. From 1909 until 1945, Korea was part of the Japanese empire, and Korean Buddhism came under the influence of Japanese schools. Buddhism has recently had to contend with challenges from other faiths, such as the Unification Church of Reverend Sung Myung Moon.

TOWARD THE ONE-POINTED MIND

Bodhidharma, founder of Zen Buddhism, brought a new form of meditative Buddhism from India to China.

After the historical Buddha, one figure towers above all others in the development of Zen Buddhism (*Ch'an* in Chinese and *Son* in Korean): the wandering Indian monk Bodhidharma (*c.* 470–534 C.E.), known as Tamo in China and Daruma in Japan. According to tradition, he was both the twenty-eighth Indian patriarch and the first Chinese patriarch of Ch'an. He left India in 517 and arrived in South China in 520 after a long, perilous journey. Little is actually known about his life, but a rich mythology of tales chronicles his arrival and stay in China. Several scholars have argued that the Bodhidharma of the Zen tradition never extisted, but rather that he is a compound figure constructed from the lives and works of the many Indian missionaries who brought the teachings of the Mahayana tradition of Buddhism, which is known as *Dhyana*, to China.

Dhyana, which means meditation or absorption, is not a purely Buddhist concept. The term occurs in the *Upanishads*, the holy texts of Hinduism, and it is also the seventh limb of the *Ashtanga* or *Raja Yoga* of Pantajali. In Hinduism,

DARUMA DOLLS

In Japan, images of Bodhidharma (Daruma) as a limbless torso with the pupils of his large, staring eyes left unpainted are commonly used as a good luck charm. Those wishing to accomplish a difficult task will purchase a Daruma doll, dedicate themselves to the task by painting in one of the eyes, and paint the second pupil only when they have achieved the task.

India is the historical home to Buddhism and today, Indian culture remains significantly influenced by the religion.

Dhyana denotes both the practice of meditation and the higher state of consciousness that precedes *Samadhi*, or final liberation from rebirth.

In Buddhism, Dhyana is also known as *Jhana*, an eight-stage process which is intended to withdraw the senses from all distractions so that the seeker may achieve "one-pointed concentration." The four lower Jhanas are meditations on forms, and the four higher Jhanas proceed to meditations on the formless. Jhana is not an end in itself, but an impermanent state. Although they are profoundly powerful experiences in themselves, they act only as a means of achieving the tranquility and insight needed to gain enlightenment.

The successors of Bodhidharma, the Chinese patriarchs, developed Dhyana into Ch'an Buddhism, integrating it with the native Taoist philosophy of Laotzu. It was taken to Korea with other forms of Chinese Buddhism, where it was known as Son, and finally reached Japan in the seventh century.

"NOTHING IS HOLY!"

Legend and fact intertwine in Bodhidharma's life to illuminate his profound understanding of the nature of reality.

In this traditional Chinese representation, Bodhidharma is shown as a fierce-looking figure with bushy beard and eyebrows.

BODHIDHARMA AND THE EMPEROR WU

When Bodhidharma arrived in China, he was summoned to appear at the southern court of the Emperor Wu (c. 502–550 C.E.), a generous patron of Mahayana Buddhism. The emperor asked Bodhidharma what merit he had earned from his many good works.

"None at all," Bodhidharma replied.

Perplexed, the emperor asked, "What then is the meaning of the holy truths?"

"Emptiness. Nothing is holy," came the reply.

Exasperated and confused, the emperor asked, "Who is facing me?"

"I do not know," Bodhidharma replied.

This encounter can be seen as one of the first Zen stories, and Bodhidharma's answers to the emperor anticipate the future teaching style of the Ch'an and Zen masters. Not only is

Bodhidharma an iconoclast by finding no merit in the emperor's many good works, but he also rejects any scholastic transmission of Dharma through the study of the scriptures.

BODHIDHARMA AND THE SHAOLIN TEMPLE

Finding little understanding in Southern China, Bodhidharma traveled north to the kingdom of Wei, going to a mountain cave in Loyang near the Shaolin Temple. He found the monks of the temple to be holy and strong in mind, but woefully weak in body. They did not have the physical stamina for the many hours of meditation that Dhyana required. He taught them a series of exercises, which became the basis for Shaolin Lohan boxing, the reputed origin of all Chinese kung fu.

It is said that after nine years immobile in meditation, Bodhidharma's legs and arms had withered away. Another legend tells that he pulled off his own eyebrows to prevent himself from nodding off as he meditated. Tea bushes are said to have sprouted from where they fell. His successors used the less extreme method of drinking tea to keep awake during meditation.

Buddhism has a long association with the martial arts of China and Japan. Tradition has it that Bodhidharma's teachings form the basis of Chinese kung fu. Latter-day Shaolin monks demonstrate their skill (above).

"BRING ME YOUR MIND"

Bodhidharma is acknowledged to be the first in a line of six Chinese patriarchs of Ch'an Buddhism.

While Bodhidharma sat in meditation facing the cave wall—a current practice of Soto Zen known as *mempeki*—a renowned scholar of the day, Hui-k'o (478–593 C.E.), came to the cave to beg for instruction. The first patriarch ignored Hui-k'o and continued to meditate.

In desperation, Hui-k'o cut off his own arm with a sword and presented it to Bodhidharma, saying, "Your disciple's mind is not at peace. I beg you to give it peace."

Bodhidharma replied, "Bring me your mind and I will set it at peace." Hui-k'o said, "I have searched for my mind, but I cannot find it."

"There, I have set it at rest for you," Bodhidharma said. And, with those words, Hui-k'o became enlightened. Hui-k'o remained with Bodhidharma and received instruction for six more years.

When Bodhidharma decided to return to India, he questioned his disciples to see who was worthy to be his successor. While the other disciples gave clever answers to Bodhidharma's question, Hui-k'o stood in silence. Bodhidharma appointed Hui-k'o as the second patriarch of Ch'an. During the rule of the third patriarch, Seng-ts'an (d. 606 C.E.), Ch'an was influenced by Taoism. Seng-ts'an is the author of a poem whose opening lines express this union:

> Hui-k'o's self-mutilation with a sword was an example of the often violent lengths to which Zen masters were prepared to go in their pursuit of enlightenment.

The Perfect Way is not difficult,
It only refuses to express preferences.
Only when freed from hate and love,
It reveals itself fully and without concealment.

(Trans. D.T. Suzuki, *Essays in Zen Buddhism*; London: Rider, 1970)

The fourth patriarch, Tao-hsin (580–651 C.E.), founded the first monastic community, which

The great masters of Ch'an, and later of Zen, often preferred the solitude of the hermitage to the comfort of the cloister.

became the model for successive monasteries in China and Japan, and emphasized the value of *zazen*, or sitting meditation. The fifth patriarch, Hung-jen (601–674 C.E.), advocated progressive control of the mind through meditation, especially by concentrating on the figure one, a single horizontal stroke in the Chinese writing system, which became a common theme in later Ch'an and Zen calligraphy. The Golden Age of Ch'an was ushered in by the sixth and last undisputed patriarch, whose succession was also responsible for a division within Ch'an. This division subsequently led to the emergence of the Northern and Southern schools.

CHINESE FIGURES

Regular Chinese characters for numbers use relatively few strokes. The characters for the numbers one, two, and three are just one, two, and three horizontal strokes respectively. A more complicated series of numbers does also exist but the simplicity of form (as shown below) lends itself to a starting-point for meditation, as well as a basis and inspiration for Zen calligraphy,

THE LAST
PATRIARCH

Of humble birth, the sixth patriarch's appointment caused the division of Ch'an into two rival schools.

The sixth and last patriarch of Ch'an was Hui-neng, or Wei-lang (638–713 C.E.). He began life as an illiterate gatherer of firewood in southern China. One day, when he heard a recitation of the *Diamond Sutra* (or teaching), he experienced a deep spiritual awakening and decided to find a teacher. He traveled north to see the fifth patriarch, Hung-jen, who was the abbot of a large monastery, and asked him for instruction. At first, Hung-jen did not

Listening to a recitation of the *Diamond Sutra* (shown below) was a profoundly spiritual experience for Hui-neng. He is said to have been the posthumous author of the *Platform Sutra*, despite the fact that he was, apparently, completely illiterate.

take Hui-neng seriously, but was impressed by his depth of understanding. He could not, however, allow an illiterate peasant to become a monk, so set him to work in the kitchen. Several months later, when Hung-jen was looking for a successor he asked the monks to summarize their knowledge of Ch'an in a poem. As all the monks expected the abbot's successor to be the senior monk, Shen-hsiu (667–730 C.E.), Hui-neng was the only one to write a poem. It read:

> Ch'an, like Zen, teaches not through sutras, but through stories, such as Hui-neng's lesson about the flag.

> The body is the tree of enlightenment,
> The mind is a clear mirror,
> At all times we must polish it
> That no dust may sully it.

Hui-neng asked a monk to read him the poem and wrote one of his own in reply:

> The mind is not like the tree of enlightenment,
> There is no clear mirror.
> From the beginning nothing exists.
> What, then, can the dust sully?

On hearing this poem, Hung-jen named him as his successor and sixth patriarch. But fearing for his life from Shen-hsiu's supporters, Hui-neng fled back to southern China. When the fifth patriarch died, Hui-neng began his ministry in the south after the following incident:

While traveling, Hui-neng came across two monks arguing about a flag. One said, "The flag is moving." The other disagreed and said, "The wind is moving." Hui-neng corrected them both by saying, "Neither the wind nor the flag are moving. It is your mind that moves."

"SUDDEN SOUTH, GRADUAL NORTH"

The great divide between Northern and Southern Ch'an Buddhism, and also Zen, concerns the best way to achieve enlightenment.

The disputed succession of the fifth patriarch, Hung-jen, ultimately led to the division of Ch'an Buddhism into two schools: the Northern, established around Shen-hsiu, Hui-neng's rival, and the Southern, from Hui-neng through to his own Dharma-successor, Shen-hui (d. 762 C.E.). The dispute was not merely personal. On the contrary, it is said that Hui-neng and Shen-hsiu themselves were on good terms, but that their disciples often came to blows. It was even claimed that the followers of the Northern school made an attempt on Hui-neng's life. How much credence can be given to such accounts is uncertain, however, since all records were written by the ultimate victors, the followers of the Southern school.

The main difference between the two schools rested in the achievement of enlightenment. The Northern school was associated with gradual enlightenment and the Southern with sudden enlightenment—an opposition summed up by the pithy Japanese aphorism, *Nanton Hokuzen* (Sudden South, Gradual North).

The northern patriarch Shen-hsiu taught a gentle path to enlightenment through study, exercises, and meditation. His line, however, lasted for only a few generations after his death.

Shen-hui formally claimed the superiority of the Southern school at a great assembly in Hua-t'ai in 732. He refused to acknowledge the Northern school as equal or complementary to the Southern, saying that there could only be one line of Dharma-succession from Bodhidharma, and that this was to his own master, Hui-neng. True enlightenment, he argued, was a sudden realization of no-mind. "All the masters achieved enlightenment in a single moment," he said. His successors employed some surprising methods to trigger that moment of realization, including shouts and blows.

Although the Southern school came to dominate Ch'an in China, the argument between gradual versus sudden enlightenment remains unresolved in Japanese Zen, where the respective views are represented by the Soto and Rinzai schools.

> Rivalries between sparring factions of the different schools were rife in Ch'an's history.

"STRANGE WORDS, EXTRAORDINARY ACTIONS"

One of the outstanding representatives of the Southern school, Ma-tsu, taught the Ch'an of sudden enlightenment.

"Strange words, extraordinary actions" sums up the teaching style of Ma-tsu Tao-i (709–788 C.E.), the third-generation leader of Hui-neng's Southern school of Ch'an. A man of fearsome presence, he became the model for later Zen masters.

Ma-tsu was the first Ch'an master to use the shout, "Ho!", and the stick, or *kyosaku* in Japanese, as a routine part of his teaching style. The ear-splitting "Ho!" not only serves to awaken the student to enlightenment at a critical moment, but also represents the wordless transmission of Dharma between master and pupil. Ma-tsu's violent methods did not end with a blow from a stick. He concluded one exchange with his successor, Pai-chang (720–814 C.E.), by pulling the younger monk's nose so hard that he yelled out in pain. However, the experience, we are told, led to Pai-chang's instant enlightenment.

Ma-tsu was a pupil of Nan-yueh (677–744 C.E.). One day when Ma-tsu was engaged in zazen (sitting meditation), Nan-yueh asked him what he was doing.

"I wish to become a Buddha," was Ma-tsu's reply.

Nan-yueh began to rub a tile together with a stone. When Ma-tsu asked what he was doing, he replied: "I am making a mirror from this tile."

Ma-tsu asked, "How can you make a mirror from a tile?"

The teacher replied, "How can you become a Buddha through zazen?" Ma-tsu's teaching is summarized in the words, "Apart from the mind there is no Buddha, apart from the Buddha, there is no mind." Enlightenment is not the fruit of years of meditation and study, but the realization of an instant.

Ma-tsu had a number of outstanding followers. His own successor, Pai-chang, established the monastic rule that is still in use today. Ma-tsu's line ended with Chao-chou (Japanese: Joshu, 778–897 C.E.), who created several famous koans, but did not find a successor. From then on, the succession of the sudden school of enlightenment would be taken over by another extraordinary Ch'an master, Lin-chi.

> Ma-tsu taught that the pursuit of enlightenment through years of zazen is as fruitless an activity as rubbing a tile and a stone together to make a mirror.

"JUST BE YOURSELF!"

*A master of the Southern school of sudden enlightenment,
Lin-chi is also honored as the founder of Japan's Rinzai-shu Zen.*

One of the most influential Ch'an masters in the line established by Hui-neng, Lin-chi (Linzi, or Rinzai Gigen, d. 866 C.E.) was a student of Huang-po Hsi-yun (d. c. 850 C.E.). For three years Lin-chi followed the routine of monastic life. But the head monk had noticed the young Lin-chi's complete lack of pride or self-interest. The monk suggested that Lin-chi request an interview with the abbot Huang-po, and ask him: "What is the meaning of Bodhidharma coming from the West?" On asking his question, the abbot hit him on the head with his stick. Despondent and confused, he sought the aid of another Ch'an teacher, Ta-yu. When he heard Lin-chi's story, Ta-yu said, "How kind Huang-po is. He is only trying to help you." At these words, Lin-chi experienced a profound awakening and began jumping for joy, saying, "There is nothing to Huang-po's Ch'an! It's really very simple!"

Lin-chi then returned to Huang-po, who tested him in his newly-found understanding. Lin-chi hit his master and let out a great shout of "Ho!" (*Kwatz!* in Japanese). The abbot pretended to be angry, but instead of having Lin-chi ejected from the monastery, he accepted him as his disciple.

Lin-chi's Ch'an was an experience to be lived on a daily basis. He advised his students to see beyond the snares of blind desire and to embrace the vision that being ordinary will bring: "When it is time to dress, get dressed. When you must walk, walk. Do not concern yourself with becoming a

Lin-chi believed that enlightenment could only be experienced by a sudden awakening, best brought about by a sharp blow and an exclamation of "Ho!"

Lin-chi's emphasis on vision through ordinary living was central both to his philosophy and to more general Zen thought. Art—and especially art taking ordinary things and the natural world as its subject—is often considered a means to attaining insight.

Buddha, just be yourself. Though the fool may laugh at you, the wise man will understand."

A strong advocate of the "Ho!" and Kyosaku school of Ch'an, Lin-chi, when asked a metaphysical question, was most likely to reply with a shout or a well-aimed blow. His students could not respond by falling back on traditional Buddhist learning. However, if they were sincere, they were forced into new ways of thinking. Lin-chi's line spawned one of the two major schools of Zen Buddhism in Japan, the *Rinzai-shu*.

CLIMBING THE
NINE MOUNTAINS

The kingdoms of the Korean peninsula developed their own rich tradition of Ch'an Buddhism, known as Son.

Ch'an, or Son, found a home on the Korean peninsula in around 630 C.E. Its appeal, however, was not immediate. Wonhyo (618–686) laid the groundwork for its later success. He was one of Korea's leading Buddhist thinkers and founded the Popsong (Dharma-nature) school. Although not a Son Buddhist himself, Wonhyo taught a syncretic form of Buddhism that tried to reconcile different schools.

During the Silla period (668–935), the nine Son schools, or "Nine Mountains," were founded. Seven of these were derived from the line of Ma-tsu of the Southern school of Ch'an. In the succeeding Koryo period (935–1392), Chinul (1158–1210) set

The nine Son schools are represented by nine mountains, each a pinnacle of thought and teaching that would have to be integrated with its rivals.

about to reform Son and revive Korean Buddhism. He began integrating the "Nine Mountains" and reconciling the fundamental division of Ch'an Buddhism with his doctrine of "Sudden Enlightenment and Gradual Practice" (*Tono-Chomsu*).

In 1623, Korea's neo-Confucianist king forbade Buddhist monks and nuns from residing in or even entering the capital. As a result, many of Korea's Son monasteries are found in isolated mountain locations.

Chinul entered a monastery at the age of seven and was ordained at 25. He did not study formally, but had three separate awakenings while reading Son texts, including Hui-neng's *Platform Sutra*. Instead of returning to the capital to teach, he established the Songgwang Sa monastery on Mt. Chogye. Chinul advocated a doctrine that would reconcile the sudden and gradual Son schools, but his early death prevented him from uniting the various schools in Korea.

Chinul's work was taken up a century later by T'aego (1301–1382) who became enlightened at the age of 33. He completed the work that Chinul had begun and founded the Chogye school, uniting the nine Son schools. The Chogye school remains the leading force in contemporary Korean Buddhism.

CHAPTER THREE

THE
FLOWER
BLOOMS

THE FLOWER BLOOMS

Displacing the native Shinto faith, Buddhism was unchallenged as Japan's principal religion until the nineteenth-century Meiji Restoration, when it was briefly eclipsed by a Shinto revival.

Buddhism was introduced to Japan from Korea in the mid-sixth century C.E. After initial resistance from the supporters of the native Shinto, the Japanese elite adopted Buddhism: its position was consolidated when Prince Shotoku (574–664 C.E.) introduced reforms positing it as the state religion of Japan. The early Japanese schools closely imitated their Chinese models, and were from both the Hinayana and Mahayana traditions. Dosho (629–700), the founder of the Hosso school, introduced a form of Southern school Ch'an to Japan, but Zen itself would not take root for another five centuries.

Japan's imperial system, the Heian period (794–1185), saw the complexity of the Tendai and Shingon (esoteric) schools maintaining Buddhism as the official state faith. It was only during the Kamakura period (1185–1333), when the first of many dynasties of *shoguns* (military dictators), seized power, that Buddhism became a truly popular religion with the introduction of Pure Land and Nichiren, and Rinzai and Soto Zen schools.

During the long period of Japan's self-imposed isolation, known as the Edo period (1600–1867), Buddhism was closely allied to the government of the Tokugawa shoguns, who ruled Japan from Edo (now Tokyo). When the shoguns were finally overthrown and the imperial court restored, Shinto was restored as the official religion, and Buddhism was persecuted for a time.

After Japan's defeat in the Pacific War (1941–1945), the U.S. occupation authorities created a democratic, secular political system in Japan. The granting of freedom of religious belief led to the emergence of many new religions—faiths that often combined elements from different traditions: Christian, Buddhist, and Shinto. Like Ch'an in China and Son in Korea, Japanese Zen fared much better during periods of religious persecution than other Buddhist schools. It continues to thrive, attracting students from all over the world.

The colossal *Daibutsu* (Great Buddha) in Todaiji temple in the old imperial capital of Nara is a lasting testament of the power of Buddhism in ancient Japan.

THE
FOUNDER of ZEN

The Japan of the samurai warrior was the fertile soil in which Eisai planted both the teachings of Zen and the first tea bushes.

The father of Japanese Zen, Eisai (or Yosai, 1141–1215 C.E.) founded the Rinzai-shu (Chinese: Lin-chi school of Ch'an) and built the first Zen temples and monasteries in Japan. A monk of the Tendai Buddhist sect, Eisai first went to China in 1168 where he studied Chinese Buddhism and collected T'ien-t'ai (*Tendai*) scriptures. He visited China a second time in 1187, this time to study Ch'an under a master of the Lin-chi (Southern) school of sudden enlightenment. After three years of training, he achieved enlightenment and received his *inka-shomei*, or seal of recognition, which gave him the authority to teach and establish his own line.

Eisai returned to Japan in 1192, at a crucial period in his homeland's history. Seven years earlier, the first dynasty of samurai rulers of Japan, the Minamoto shoguns, had seized power from the imperial court. Eisai spent ten years in Fukuoka in the westernmost part of the country, where he founded Japan's first Zen temple, Shofukuji. There he taught a syncretic form of Zen that combined

INKA-SHOMEI

The inka-shomei is a formal recognition on the part of the roshi that his pupil has reached enlightenment. Originally, the inka would only be granted once a student had reached satori, but it is now generally accepted that there are various stages of enlightenment. Thus, it is not uncommon for inka to be granted at various stages on the journey, each stage designating the grade the student has reached. The granting of the inka-shomei can be oral or written. An example of the latter can be seen at right.

Eisai built the first Zen
monasteries in Japan
in the face of
opposition from other
Buddhist sects.

elements from Tendai,
Shingon, and Ch'an.
Despite opposition from
the powerful Tendai
school monasteries on
nearby Mt. Hiei, Eisai
succeeded in founding
Kenninji, the first Zen
monastery, and later
founded Jufukuji, a
second monastic
establishment, in the
shogun's eastern capital
of Kamakura.

One of Eisai's most
durable innovations was
the introduction of tea to Japan. He wrote the first book on tea drinking, in which
he advocated tea on health grounds, to replace *sake*, or rice wine. Green tea was
used by Zen monks to keep awake during zazen meditation practice; its making
and drinking also became the heart of the ritual of the tea ceremony, or *chanoyu*.

Eisai was a prolific and much sought-after teacher. He was greatly admired by
Dogen, the founder of the second great tradition of Japanese Zen, the *Soto-shu*.

THE
GREAT DEATH

Rinzai-shu Zen, heir to the Chinese Ch'an Southern school, follows the path to sudden enlightenment through the study of koans.

Rinzai is the Japanese name for the Lin-chi school of Ch'an Buddhism. Like other Southern-style schools, Rinzai lays great emphasis on the use of the "Kwatz!" shout, the stick, and dynamic exchanges between master and student centered around graded koans, paradoxical statements, and questions used to derail rational thought processes. All these methods are designed to bring the student to a mental crisis, at

Rinzai-shu temples and monasteries in Japan were divided in a way that echoed the corresponding earlier division of Ch'an temples in China.

which point the master can push the student into the experience of enlightenment. This moment of realization is called the "Great Death" or the "Great Doubt."

Rinzai only became recognized as an independent school of Buddhism years after Eisai's death. Formal recognition by the shogunate led to a tripartite division of Rinzai-shu temples and monasteries. The five most important temples were called the *Gozan* (Five Mountains), imitating the Chinese division of Ch'an temples. The constituent temples of the Gozan changed over the centuries, but they were always found in either the imperial capital, Kyoto, or the shogunal capital of Kamakura. Next were the *Jussetsu* (Ten temples), and the *Shozan* (including other major temples, mostly outside Kyoto and Kamakura). This division is also the origin of the other name given to this school, the Gozan-shu.

Both Nampo Jomyo (1235–1308 C.E.) and his disciple Shuho Myocho (1282–1388) are leading figures in the establishment of the Rinzai-shu in Japan. Shuho Myocho, given the posthumous title Daito Kokushi, was the first abbot of Daitokuji in Kyoto, which is still one of the leading Zen centers in Japan. Daito Kokushi is famous for his unstinting self-sacrifice. Throughout his life, he suffered from lameness. When he was about to die, he forced his leg into the lotus position and, breaking it, said, "I have followed you all my life, now it is time for you to follow me." He then wrote his farewell poem and passed away.

The full lotus position demands that each foot be placed on the opposite thigh. Followers of Zen have been prepared to go to extreme lengths to achieve the perfect balance of mind and body facilitated by this meditative posture.

As with any organization having been granted state recognition and privileges, the Rinzai-shu gradually lost its original iconoclastic dynamism. By the eighteenth century, many of its abbots, monks, and nuns were time-servers who sold inka-shomei, or certificates of enlightenment. The sect was revitalized by the work of an extraordinary man, Hakuin Ekaku (1685–1768).

CREED OF THE
WARRIOR

Buddhism remained an elite court religion until the twelfth century when the shogun-led samurai seized power.

The political earthquake that brought the Kamakura shoguns to power in 1185 was not a mere shift of political power between aristocratic families. Nor was it a mere geographic shift of power from Kyoto—the imperial capital in western Japan—to Kamakura in eastern Japan. It was nothing less than a wholesale transformation of Japanese society from a centralized bureaucratic state to a land of semi-independent, rival, and feudal domains. Henceforth, the emperor and his court would be relegated to a powerless ceremonial role, while the provincial lords, or *daimyo,* who headed the samurai clans, ran the country and competed for the title of shogun.

The established Buddhist schools of the Heian period were closely allied to the imperial court, and their sophisticated theologies and complex rituals had little appeal to the provincial daimyo. Their worldly power, too, was often a threat to the shogun's authority. They were major landholders, and kept large armies of warrior-monks, which they used to intimidate the government. For these reasons, the shogun were interested in patronizing a new school of Buddhism that better reflected the samurai ideology.

Modern readers might find it unusual that a school of Buddhism, which preaches respect for all life, should be so popular among the bloodthirsty samurai. On one level, they found Zen's emphasis on self-discipline a useful adjunct to their own notions of honor, duty, and unswerving loyalty to their lord. In an uncertain and violent period, Zen's doctrines of

The Zen philosophy is very immediate: its asceticism has much in common with the warrior mentality.

living in the moment, transcending life and death, and sudden enlightenment, also had a particular appeal.

Zen was incorporated into the samurai's martial training to improve their concentration and mental endurance. The great swordsman Miyamoto Musashi (1584–1645 C.E.), who wrote the *Book of Five Rings*, taught that, in order to excel, the swordsman has to transcend his fear of death. The link with Japan's martial arts has endured to the present day; especially those associated with the samurai, such as Japanese fencing, or *kendo*, and traditional archery, or *kyudo*.

Often equated with zazen meditation, the practice of *kyudo* (Japanese archery) has a long history associating it with Zen Buddhism. Here, archers go through the complex ritual required of them prior to releasing an arrow.

SILENT
ILLUMINATION

*Contrasting with the Rinzai-shu in both practice and approach,
the Soto-shu teaches a gentle and gradual path to enlightenment.*

The second major stream of Zen teaching in Japan, the Soto-shu, was founded by
Dogen (1200–1253 C.E.). Readers will recall that Hui-neng, the sixth disputed
patriarch of Ch'an, started a line that included Lin-chi (Japanese: Rinzai), and
which culminated in the Rinzai-shu. The line of his rival for the patriarchate,

Shen-hsiu, included many
important Ch'an masters, several of
whom founded their own schools.
Tung-shan (807–869 C.E., Japanese:
Tozan) and his disciple and
successor Ts'ao-shan (840–901,
Japanese: Sozan) were co-founders
of the Ts'ao-tung school (made up
of the first characters of the names
of the founders; Japanese: *Soto*).
Tung-shan was a
contemporary of Lin-chi, but his
approach to teaching was
completely different. In contrast to
Lin-chi's "shout-and-stick" Zen, he
stressed the importance of zazen—
sitting meditation—and an intuitive
understanding of enlightenment.
The difference in approach was

Zazen sitting meditation lies at the
very heart of Soto Zen teaching
and practice.

The quiet, contemplative approach of Soto-shu Zen has the greatest appeal, both in Japan and in the West.

transplanted to Japan, by Eisai, founder of Rinzai-shu, and Dogen, founder of the Soto-shu. Although their interpretations of Buddhism are similar, the two schools approach training very differently. Where Rinzai stresses koan introspection, and meditation as focuses to enlightenment, Soto uses few koans, and teaches *mokusho zen*—silent illumination through *shikantaza*, in which the act of zazen itself is associated with the enlightened state.

Two monastic establishments, Eiheiji and Sojiji, are recognized as the headquarters of the Soto-shu. Sojiji, rebuilt in Yokohama after a fire destroyed it in 1898, is the larger of the two, with many subtemples all over Japan and about 15,000 meditation centers worldwide. The rivalry between the two monasteries led to many difficulties for the Soto-shu, which were only resolved in the end of the nineteenth century. The sect saw a revival in the seventeenth and, again, in the twentieth century, with reforms aiming to restore the original monastic rule established by Dogen.

THE DROPPING AWAY OF THE BODY

"Just sit quietly and you will become enlightened"
is the heart of Dogen's Soto-shu Zen.

Dogen (1200–1253 C.E.), founder of the Soto-shu, was orphaned as a child, experiencing early the suffering of the transience of life. His mother's dying wish was that he become a monk, and, at the age of 13, he joined one of the Tendai monasteries on Mt. Hiei. But after only one year of training, he experienced great doubt. Why, if we all have Buddha-nature, he asked himself, is it so hard to realize it? Dissatisfied with the Tendai school, he left and sought another teacher. Some speculate that after a long search, he met Myozen, a disciple of Eisai, the founder of the Rinzai-shu in Japan, who began to teach him about the Zen

> Dogen's harsh meditation regime was, in the end, a hindrance rather than a help in his pursuit of enlightenment.

Dogen's Zen postulates metaphorical as well as physical obstacles to enlightenment. The very desire for satori can itself be an obstacle to its attainment.

conception of enlightenment. Dogen studied for eight years with Myozen.

At the age of 24, Dogen went to China where he studied with Ju-ching (1163–1128) of the Ts'ao-tung school, who advocated extended periods of zazen meditation practice. He is said to have begun meditating at 2:30 A.M. and finished at 11:00 P.M. Dogen adopted this grueling regime, but soon fell into the error of meditating passively rather than actively.

One day he overheard Ju-ching upbraiding another disciple who was not meditating, but merely dozing.

"The practice of zazen is not mere sitting!" Ju-ching said. "It is the dropping away of the mind and body. What do you think you can accomplish by dozing?"

This remark triggered a deep understanding in Dogen about the nature of zazen and enlightenment. He described the experience in the following terms: "Mind and body dropped away. This should be experienced by everyone. It is like trying to fill a bottomless basket or fill a bottomless cup—no matter how much you fill it, it will never be full."

Returning to Japan, he set up a meditation hall, or *zendo*, in Kyoto. In Dogen's Zen, there is no need to struggle for enlightenment; in fact, the desire for it is itself an obstacle to its realization. According to the shikantaza form of zazen, enlightenment will come as a natural result of meditation.

THE SON OF THE WANDERING CLOUD

The eccentric Rinzai-shu master, Ikkyu, is also recognized as one of Japan's most accomplished painters, poets, and calligraphers.

With its uncompromising, sometimes violent style, Rinzai-shu Zen has spawned many extraordinary characters. None more so than Ikkyu Sojun (1394–1481 C.E.). Ikkyu was said to be the illegitimate son of the Emperor Go-Komatsu (1377–1433). As a child, he was sent to a Zen monastery as protection from court intrigue. He left the monastery at age 16, disgusted by the greed and corruption into which Zen had fallen. He chose to continue his studies with masters who were known for their strictness: Ken'o (d. 1414) and Kaso (1352–1428). It was during his time with Kaso that he finally experienced enlightenment. He had gone to meditate on a boat on Lake Biwa, when he was disturbed by the cawing of a crow. He wrote the following poem about the event:

For ten years I was in turmoil,
Seething and angry, but now my time
*   has come!*
The crow caws, an arhat emerges
*   from the filth,*
And in the sunlight of Chao-yang, a
*   jade beauty sings.*

(Trans. John Stevens, *Three Zen Masters*; Tokyo, New York: Kodsansha Internationonal, 1993)

The cawing of a crow disturbed Ikkyu's meditation, but was the trigger for his ultimate enlightenment.

The tradition of
ink-wash painting in
which Ikkyu excelled
is continued today
by latter-day students
of Zen.

When Kaso tried to
award him his inka-
shomei, or certificate of
enlightenment, Ikkyu
hurled it to one side, refusing to have anything to do with the corrupt practices of
the Zen establishment. He preferred to live the life of a wanderer, and called
himself "the son of a wandering cloud."

Ikkyu is famous in Japan for his eccentric behavior. On the New Year's Day
holiday in 1440, he appeared in the streets of Kyoto carrying a bamboo pole with
a skull on the top, and crying, "Beware! Beware!" When the citizens reproached
him, he answered, "Reminders of death should not spoil your celebrations. I am
celebrating, too."

At age 80, he finally accepted one of the most senior Zen abbacies, that of
Daitokuji in Kyoto, which had been destroyed by fire. He only accepted the post
because he wanted to see the monastery rebuilt. But, to the end, he was an
uncompromising foe of corruption and sham Zen. Ikkyu is also considered to be
one of Japan's most accomplished poets, calligraphers, and ink painters.

THE GREAT
REFORMER

The great master Hakuin reformed the Rinzai-shu and began the codification of the koan into a teaching method.

The man who revitalized the Rinzai-shu and opened Zen teaching to Japan's emerging middle class during the Edo period (1600–1867 C.E.) was Hakuin Ekaku (1686–1769). Despite the opposition of his parents, he became a monk at the age of 15. While he was studying, he was deeply disturbed by the story of the murder of the Ch'an master, Yen-t'ou Ch'uan-huo (828–887), who had let out a great cry of anguish as he died. He persevered, however, and after four years of work on the koan of Joshu's dog, he had an experience which he himself took to be final enlightenment, or satori. He described it as, "Freezing in an ice field thousands of leagues wide, and within, a sense of utmost clarity."

Blinded by his pride, Hakuin asked his abbot to confirm his enlightenment, but the latter refused to do so. Hakuin went to another master, but he, too, was skeptical. He persevered and true illumination came to him when he was out begging for alms. Stopping in front of a house, he did not hear the occupant, an old woman, say she had nothing for him. Incensed that he was still standing there, the old woman struck Hakuin a fierce blow, knocking him senseless. When he awoke, his mind was clear and he understood the meaning of Yen-t'ou's cry. "Yen-t'ou is fit, strong, and well," he said. Hakuin's experience of enlightenment showed that it was not a single event that completed Zen training, but that it can be experienced several times—each time deepening the student's understanding.

After a bout of illness, Hakuin began his own career as a teacher. A man of boundless energy even in old age, he reformed the monastic rule that is followed in Rinzai temples to the present day. He created several well-known koans, including the famous, "What is the sound of one hand clapping?" and his heirs went on to codify and grade the exisiting koans. Hakuin is also acknowledged to be one of Japan's leading Zen calligraphers, painters, and poets.

Hakuin believed that he had attained enlightenment inspired by his work on the koan of Joshu's dog. His abbot refused to confirm this until he experienced true illumination while begging for alms.

BIG FOOL

Zen masters were not all terrifying eccentrics who bullied their students. Ryokan exemplifies the gentler way of Soto-shu Zen.

The fierce Hakuin and the eccentric Ikkyu represent one type of Zen master, closely associated with the Rinzai-shu. But Japan's other Zen school, the Soto-shu, has also produced some extraordinary teachers. One such was the monk, poet, and calligrapher, Ryokan Taigu (1758–1831 C.E.). Ryokan was a quiet, studious child who was sent to a Confucian academy at the age of ten. As a young man, he experienced a deep spiritual crisis and suddenly decided to become a monk. He entered Koshoji, the local Soto-shu temple, as a novice, where he remained for several years. In 1780, Kokusen (d. 1791) visited Ryokan's temple and impressed the young monk so much that he decided to become his disciple. He remained at Kokusen's temple in Tamashima (Okayama prefecture), where he studied Zen poetry, and calligraphy. Kokusen's approach to Zen was very down to earth; he described it as, "Piling stones and hauling dirt."

In 1790, he received his inka-shomei from Kokusen, certifying that he was enlightened. With his ordination as a monk came the name he was to be known by, Ryokan Taigu. Ryokan means "good and warm-hearted," and Taigu, "great fool," because he had a child-like simplicity and guilessness.

As Kokusen's Dharma-successor, Ryokan could have become the abbot of one of the great Soto-shu temples, but he preferred the life of the wanderer and hermit. He lived entirely from the alms he managed to beg, writing poetry and creating masterpieces of calligraphy. He finally reached his home province of Echigo, and settled in an old hermitage, the Gogoan,

Ryokan, who loved animals and children, preferred the solitary life of a simple hermit—writing poetry, painting, and practicing calligraphy— to the hustle of life in a great Zen temple.

that had been built on the grounds of Kokujoji temple. In his simplicity, poverty, and love of children and animals, Ryokan is often compared to Saint Francis of Assisi, another of God's fools.

His last poem reads:

> *What will remain as my legacy*
> *Flowers in the spring*
> *The cuckoo in summer*
> *And the crimson leaves*
> *Of autumn.*
>
> (Trans. John Stevens, *Three Zen Masters*)

Ryokan's love of the natural world was the starting point for much of his work, his last poem taking crimson autumn leaves as its inspiration.

CHAPTER FOUR

THE PETALS OF THE FLOWER

THE PETALS OF THE FLOWER

In contrast to the dualism of Western thought that separates good from evil, mind from body, Eastern philosophies stress the underlying oneness of reality.

Zen presents particular problems for the Western mind, which is heir to two very distinct traditions. On the one hand, there is the rational mind, which seeks scientific evidence and proof for all phenomena and experience. Rationality has its roots in the materialism and logic of the ancient Greek philosophers. This tradition believes in a world of very solid matter, governed by predictive laws. Although Relativity, Quantum, and Chaos have dislodged the old Newtonian certainties in the scientific community, for the man and woman in the street, if an object looks like a chair and you can sit on it, then it must be a chair. The world is real because we can touch it, move through it, and predict what it will do.

In complete contrast to this tradition is the Western concept of faith—"God moves in mysterious ways." He is ineffable and unknowable, and our only recourse is a blind, unquestioning faith in

To the Western mind, a chair must be a chair because we can perceive it sensorily. This broadly rational stance can conflict with religious beliefs. Eastern religions go some way to resolving this conflict.

Him if we are to win salvation. There seems to be no way to reconcile these diametrical opposites. Our culture, more than any other, works in paired opposites: good and evil, masculine and feminine, "I" and the world. Our very identities are tied up by defining what we are and what we are not.

Eastern philosophies and religions, though they sometimes employ dualities such as good and evil, look beyond them to the undifferentiated substrata of human existence that is sometimes referred to as God. In Hinduism, Taoism, and Buddhism, we are all part of the One Mind, to which we are destined to return when we have reached the correct spiritual state. In Ch'an and Zen, that state is not deferred to some future life or other worldly paradise; it is achievable in the present. Enlightenment is a lived experience that requires both great faith and great doubt, and, although it cannot be comprehended rationally, it can be proved to exist by your own experience of it.

Before we continue to examine Zen principles in more detail, we should tackle the most common criticism that Buddhism and Zen have been subjected to in their history: that they are nihilistic in outlook—life-hating faiths. While Buddhists reject the suffering of the human condition, they do not reject the human condition itself. Zen, in particular, teaches us to live completely in the moment, and because no actions have more or less value, our work, pastimes, and daily interactions are all part and parcel of the Zen life.

YIN & YANG

Yin and yang represent two poles of being which are opposite, but complementary. Yin represents femininity—everything that is withdrawn, receptive, and dark—and yang, masculinity—representing everything light, expansive, and forceful. The interaction of the two is shown by a circle divided into black and white sections with spots of the opposite color in the corresponding portion. This concept exemplifies the tendency of Eastern religions to look beyond simple dualities and see the oneness of being which, in Zen, constitutes enlightenment.

"DIRECT POINTING TO THE MIND"

Zen cannot be taught but the experience of it can be shared,
so its transmission from master to pupil is called "wordless."

A special transmission outside the scriptures,
Not founded on words and letters.
By pointing directly to the mind,
It allows us to penetrate the nature of things and attain Buddha-nature.

These famous lines, attributed to Bodhidharma, encapsulate the idea of direct or wordless transmission that is central to both Ch'an and Zen Buddhism. Transmission refers both to the transfer of authority from patriarch to patriarch, as well as to the teaching from master to disciple, when the latter achieves enlightenment. The act does not depend on any holy text, nor is it something that can be expressed in words. The transmission, however, is not some kind of mystic transfer of energy or power. It is merely symbolic of a shared understanding about the nature of reality.

The following incident from the life of the Buddha is given as the first occurrence of direct transmission: one day when the *sangha*, or community of believers, had gathered at Vulture Peak to hear the Buddha speak, he sat in silence for a long time. At length, he held up a flower. Among the Buddha's followers, only one man, Mahakashyapa, understood the Buddha's actions and smiled at his teacher. In that silent moment, the Buddha was said to have transmitted his authority to Mahakashyapa, who, upon the

The Buddha's silent flower sermon was the first wordless transmission.

64

Buddha's death, became his successor and the first Indian patriarch.

This transmission, or Dharma-succession, proceeded along the line of the 27 Indian patriarchs to Bodhidharma, and the five Ch'an patriarchs who succeeded him. In early Ch'an, the transmission from patriarch to patriarch was symbolized by the handing over of the patriarch's robe and bowl, which were said to have been used by the Buddha himself. Direct transmission explains the importance of lineage in the Dharma-succession in Ch'an and Zen, and the divisions that occurred in Ch'an after the disputed election of the sixth patriarch (see Northern and Southern schools). In later Zen, transmission was confirmed by the issuing of an inka-shomei, or certificate of enlightenment, to students who were deemed to have successfully completed their training.

The Vulture Peak, where direct transmission took place for the first time, has become a subject for many Zen artists.

WHEN IS A CHAIR
NOT A CHAIR?

Nothing we can see, hear, or touch in the world has any permanent existence. It will, of necessity, pass away.

One of the central concepts in Buddhism is "emptiness" (*sunyata* in Sanskrit, *ku* in Japanese), which states that all forms or appearances in the universe are empty. To explain what this means, let us take a common object such as a chair. The common sense view of the phenomenal world—the world of things and events that makes up what we call observable reality—is that all objects have permanent and unique natures. So, common sense says, a chair is always a chair.

However, if we take larger and larger microscopes to examine our chair, the greater the magnification, the less separate it becomes from its surroundings. At the molecular level, the boundaries of the chair, the air around it, and the person sitting on it are blurred. We cannot tell where one begins and the others end. At the atomic level, matter looks like solar systems, with vast empty gulfs separating the spinning electrons orbiting the atomic nuclei. At the subatomic level, distinctions between matter and energy are themselves abolished. Particles, which sometimes behave like minute packets of matter and, at others like oscillating waves, wink in and out of existence.

Even on the macrocosmic level of everyday life, however, a chair is not always a chair. If you were to look at a chair in time, you would see that it was once a piece of wood from a tree. Where in the tree is the chair that will be made from it? During its existence, wear and tear on the chair will change its appearance and structure: losing some of its wood and gaining deposits of dirt. In time, the chair will break, and the wood will decay, rot, and, finally, fall to dust. The chair, then, was a very temporary manifestation and its materials in themselves never possessed any innate "chairness."

Our failure to accept the idea that all things are empty and transient is the main cause of human suffering. The intellectual understanding of "emptiness" is a relatively straightforward exercise, but the aim of Zen training is to make someone both know, and personally experience, emptiness.

> Zen upsets our preconceived ideas about the true essence of objects.

"BUDDHA IS MIND, MIND IS BUDDHA"

The human personality itself, the ego to which Westerners cling to so strongly, is also an illusion.

If an inanimate object, such as a chair, is empty of form, then we, who are forever changing from moment to moment both physically and mentally—in time and space—are even less likely to possess a permanent, immortal soul or personality. In the *Heart Sutra*, the Buddha Avalokiteshvara (*Kannon* in Japanese) sees that the five conditions, or *skandas*, that constitute all human beings (form, sensation, mental activity, perception, and consciousness) are equally empty. This is a restatement of the Buddha's doctrine of *anatman*, or no-self, and explains why, when the Emperor Wu asked Bodhidharma, "Who is standing before me?" the monk replied, "I do not know."

Emptiness, however, is not synonymous with the void. Buddhism is not a nihilistic religion that leaves men and women stranded on the edge of the abyss of hopeless absurdity. There is an underlying principle in the universe, although it is devoid of form. This concept, which comes closest in Buddhism to the ideas of the Christian soul, the Holy Spirit, and God, is Buddha-nature—*Buddhata* in Sanskrit and *Bussho* in Japanese. Buddha-nature is neither neutral nor amoral, but embodies the virtues of compassion and wisdom.

When the Empress Wu asked the third patriarch of the Hua-yen school of Buddhism, Fa-tsang (643–712 C.E.), to explain Buddha-nature, he brought with him a statue of a lion made of pure gold. The lion, he explained, represented the phenomenal world that we all experience, but the gold from which it was cast was the underlying principle—Buddha-nature—which has no form of its own.

The Mahayana tradition, which includes Zen, teaches that all beings are composed of Buddha-nature, thus all of us have the same access to enlightenment, no matter who we are or what spiritual state we are in; only the fog created by our own illusions prevents us from realizing it.

Buddha-mind knows neither subject nor object, but focuses upon concepts which are beyond the man-made—and therefore illusory— limitations of form.

"I VOW TO SAVE THE COUNTLESS SENTIENT BEINGS"

The highest attainment in Mahayana Buddhism is that of the bodhisattva, who vows to free all sentient beings.

The accusation that Buddhists withdraw from the world, selfishly to pursue their own liberation, has often been made. In the Hinayana/ Theravada tradition, there can be only one Buddha in each historical cycle, and he has already appeared in the shape of Siddharta Gautama. The highest level the disciple can aspire to is that of *arhat* (Chinese: *lo-han*, Japanese: *rakan*), which precedes full Buddhahood. For the followers of the Mahayana tradition, this is an incomplete understanding of the Buddha's teaching, and indeed a limited form of Buddhism. They aspire instead to the state of bodhisattva (Chinese: *p'u-sa*, Japanese: *bosatsu*), which can be translated as "enlightenment-being."

The bodhisattva consciously turns away from his own liberation, or nirvana, which is the goal of the arhat, and remains in the world to devote his or her

The bodhisattva ideal—the subject of this painting—is central to Zen aspiration. Not content simply to achieve their own enlightenment, the bodhisattva will continue on their quest working to enable others to reach similar states of Buddhahood.

This bodhisattva's stance exemplifies the marriage of compassion and profound wisdom to which Zen Buddhists ultimately aspire.

life to helping others achieve enlightenment. Through practice of the Six Perfections, or *Paramitas*—generosity, morality, patience, effort, meditation, and wisdom—they seek to unite compassion and wisdom.

The bodhisattva ideal is at the heart of all Zen practice, and is symbolized by the recitation of the "Four Great Vows," or *Shiguzeigan*, at the end of all zazen or sitting meditation practice:

> *Shujo muhen seigando*
> (Sentient beings are numberless; I vow to save them all).
> *Bonno mujin seigandan*
> (Passions are countless; I vow to eradicate them all).
> *Homon muryo seigangaku*
> (Dharma-gates are numberless; I vow to enter them all).
> *Butsudon mujo seiganjo*
> (The way of the Buddha is without compare; I vow to realize it).

There are different forms of bodhisattvas. Anyone taking the bodhisattva vow, and who has dedicated his life to saving others, is considered to be a bodhisattva, but there are also celestial bodhisattvas. One of the most popular in East Asia is Avalokiteshvara (Japanese: Kannon, Chinese: Kuan-yin, "he/she who hears the sound of the world"). In China and Japan, Avalokiteshvara, who represents the ideal of compassion, takes female form

INTO THE LIGHT

Enlightenment is the aim of Zen, but it is not its endgame, rather the beginning of a new life.

Enlightenment—(Japanese: *kensho* or satori)—can be triggered by any number of agents. These include sudden external stimuli—a cawing crow, the ringing of a bell, or a sharp blow on the head—as well as the gradual internal process of sitting meditation. Certain schools, notably Korean Son, teach that the insight gained from a sudden experience must be deepened gradually through zazen.

For several non-Zen Buddhist schools, enlightenment is like the Christian paradise—a future reward for a life well-lived—but in Zen, satori is something to be experienced in the present. Also known as the "Great Death," enlightenment is not the endgame of Zen, but rather an awakening to our own and the universe's true nature, or Buddha-nature, and the beginning of a new, richer kind of life.

The popular image of enlightenment is that of a blissful, but essentially passive, state. But scientific evidence gathered on people in meditative states reveals that their brains, while at peace, are totally alert and alive.

Zen recognizes that there is more than one kind of enlightenment experience. While the student is meditating, he or she may experience power of mind (Japanese: *joriki*), an essentially positive state, in which the mind balances itself, bringing great joy and energy. Some believe that joriki gives access to supernatural powers, such as levitation and telepathy. Joriki, however, is merely a stage toward enlightenment. Less desirable are devil phenomena (Japanese: *makyo*)—hallucinations, which, though harmless, can be disturbing. Again, the sitter is instructed to ignore them. The first experience of enlightenment is known as kensho (seeing nature), and is the prelude to further experiences, which will deepen the seeker's understanding. The ultimate experience of satori is called *mujodo no taigen* (the embodiment of the unsurpassable way), which is the permanent experience of satori during one's earthly life.

A monkey offers a peach—a symbol of sexual enjoyment—to a devotee, who contemplates the temptation. This painting is meant to be upon the *pipalla*, or leaf of the bodhi tree, beneath which the Buddha attained enlightenment.

BREAKING THE CHAIN OF
CAUSE AND EFFECT

Through self-delusion, we increase our karmic load,
which keeps us trapped in the world of appearances.

The doctrine of Karma (Japanese: *Innen*), the law of cause and effect, is a well-known feature of Eastern religions. In Hinduism, the result of evil actions is impediment of our spiritual progress in future lives. If our karmic load is great, we risk being reborn as animals or in one of the many hells. In Buddhism, there is no soul (*anatman*) to tarnish; the effect of our evil deeds simply holds us back from realizing our Buddha-nature.

Greed, lust, and anger—sins in the Christian faith—are seen in Buddhism as errors keeping us trapped in the phenomenal world. But good actions are also sometimes to be avoided because they, too, tie us to the world. The emphasis in Zen is not the action itself, but the intention behind it. Only actions or intentions free from desire, hate, and delusion have no karmic consequences.

Once the student of Zen has taken the Bodhisattva vows, he follows the Ten Grave Precepts, or *Jujukai*, which govern his behavior. Despite their superficial similarity, these are not the Ten Commandments of Mosaic Law. To disobey them is not a sin, but an act of ignorance that will increase an individual's karmic load. The precepts are a stage on the path to realizing our Buddha-nature by reducing our karmic encumbrance. Once enlightened, we follow them not out of duty, but spontaneously. There is no inevitability or predestination in the Buddhist doctrine of Karma, as once enlightened, we break the chain of cause and effect.

THE TEN GRAVE PRECEPTS

I vow not to kill • I vow not to steal • I vow not to engage in damaging sexual behavior • I vow not to lie • I vow not to use intoxicating substances • I vow not to speak of the faults of others • I vow not to be proud of myself and defame others • I vow not to be reluctant in helping others find enlightenment • I vow not to give way to anger • I vow not to defame the Three Treasures (Buddha, Dharma, and Sangha)

Zen emphasizes intention rather than action, meaning that the acts of meditation and contemplation are themselves more important than their objects.

"IS THAT SO?"

Like the parables of Jesus, short, seemingly simple stories convey the deepest and most complex meanings.

Ch'an and Zen have little time for scriptures and learned commentaries. Both traditions are opposed to book learning and have no patience for the reverence of holy writ.

However, the Zen master, or *roshi*, needs material to illustrate his lessons. Over the centuries, a corpus of Zen stories has emerged, some of which have made their way into anthologies, such as the *Shasekishu* (*Collection of Stone and Sand*). This was compiled by the Rinzai-shu monk, Ichien (also known as Dokyo or Muju, 1226–1312 C.E.), and is still used for training today. The stories are usually short and illuminate how a follower of Zen should behave in the world.

The themes of Zen stories come from a variety of sources. Events from the life of the historical Buddha are common, but mostly they are taken from the lives of the Chinese patriarchs and Zen masters. A Japanese favorite is the life of Hakuin, the eighteenth century monk-reformer.

IS THAT SO?

Hakuin had a reputation among his neighbors for living a pure life. A beautiful girl whose parents owned a shop lived nearby. One day, her parents discovered that she was pregnant. They were furious and, when they asked her who the father was, she named Hakuin. The angry parents immediately went to see the monk to confront him. He listened patiently, and the only thing he said was, "Is that so?"

After the child was born, the parents gave him to his putative father. Hakuin took the baby in, and cared for him as best he could. Although his reputation had been ruined, he did not seem to mind. A year went by, and the girl could not stand it any longer. She admitted that the father was not Hakuin, but a young man from the town.

The parents immediately went to Hakuin to beg his pardon and retrieve the child. Hakuin gave them the child. Again, his only words were: "Is that so?"

Hakuin's equanimity extended to upholding the honor of the local girl who accused him of fathering her child.

"FIRST EMPTY YOUR CUP"

The contents of Zen stories are as old as Buddhism itself, and, at the same time, highly contemporary, for they are still being written.

Zen stories deal with a variety of themes, including some which might not appear in the anthologies of some religions, such as sex.

A CUP OF TEA

Nanin was a Zen master of Japan's Meiji period (1868–1912 C.E.). One day, he had an interview with a university professor who was interested in learning about Zen. As is the custom in Japan, Nanin offered his guest a cup of green tea. He poured his visitor a full cup, but continued pouring so that the cup overflowed. The professor cried out, "It's full! No more will go in!" Nanin set the pot down and said, "Like this cup, your mind is full of your own opinions and speculations. How can I show you Zen if you do not first empty your cup?"

Nanin's image of a cup full of green tea represented the mind full of worldly desires and concerns.

THE BLACK-NOSED BUDDHA

A nun made a statue of the Buddha and covered it with gold leaf. Wherever she went, she carried her Buddha with her. One day, she stopped at a country temple where there were several Buddhas, each in

its own niche. The nun wanted to offer incense to her Buddha alone, so she made a funnel that directed the incense smoke to her statue. As a result, the Buddha's nose became blackened with soot, making it particularly ugly.

NO LOVING KINDNESS

For 20 years, an old Chinese woman had supported a Ch'an monk. She had built a hut for him and fed him as he meditated. One day, she decided to test him to see how far he had progressed.

She asked one of the prettiest village girls to go and embrace him and ask him, "What now?"

The girl did exactly as she was told, entering his hut and caressing him. "What will you do now?" she asked.

The monk replied frostily, "An old tree grows on a cold winter rock. Nowhere is there any warmth."

In the story of the black-nosed Buddha, the nun directed incense to her own Buddha so that she could worship it alone.

The girl reported what had taken place to the old woman.

The old woman was furious. "To think that I have fed him for 20 years!" she said. "He showed no consideration for your need, spared no effort to explain your condition. He did not have to show passion, but he should have shown some compassion."

She immediately went to the hut, and, after evicting the monk, burned it to the ground.

THE TEN BULLS

A defining characteristic of Zen is its use of the pictorial arts to convey its message in a simple and immediate fashion.

In addition to the koans and teachings contained in stories about the patriarchs, Zen makes use of the immediacy of the pictorial arts to convey its message. The Ten Bulls (also known as the *Ox-Herding Sequence*) is a series of paintings of the Song-Dynasty (969–1276 C.E.) Ch'an master Kakuan, who was a follower of the Lin-chi school of Ch'an. The sequence represents the various stages of Zen life, using the metaphor of a boy who goes in search of his lost bull. The bull represents Buddha-nature, and the boy, the human being. In the first part of the sequence, the boy and the bull are separate entities, but as the series progresses, they become one.

THE SEARCH FOR THE BULL
The bull has been lost, symbolic of the loss of spirituality. Because of his separation from Buddha-nature, and the delusion caused by his senses, the boy cannot find the bull.

DISCOVERING THE FOOTPRINTS
Despite his own confusion, the boy discovers the bull's footprints with the help of the scriptures (sutras).

PERCEIVING THE BULL
The boy's true nature is opened through sound. He sees into the origins of things, and his senses are calmed and become harmonious.

得牛四

CATCHING THE BULL
The boy has caught the
bull, but it is difficult to
control and wants to
return to the pastures it
found. The boy has to
assert control by
being strict.

牧牛五

TAMING THE BULL
At length, the bull comes
under control, and the
boy can lead him
without trouble.

歸家騎牛六

RIDING THE BULL HOME
The struggle is over. The
boy has transcended gain
and loss. He rides on the
back of the now tamed
bull, playing his flute.
His heart is filled with
incomparable joy.

The bull is one of the most common and useful domestic animals in China, and its symbolic and practical importance would have been immediately apparent to Kakuan's audience. The series is modeled on an earlier, Taoist eight-bull series, but Kakuan's Ten Bulls are purely Zen. Each bull is accompanied by a short verse and prose commentary. The series has been reproduced many times in China and Japan.

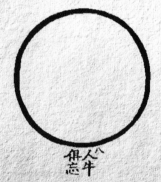

THE BULL TRANSCENDED
The boy is alone. He no longer sees the bull as separate from himself and recognizes the bull as a symbol that he no longer needs. He is now whole and at peace.

BOTH BULL AND SELF TRANSCENDED
Both the boy and the bull have vanished, and not even the concept of holiness remains. In this empty state, the fullness of life can be experienced.

REACHING THE SOURCE
The boy remains in the immovable mind. He perceives the world as it is, in constant flux—rivers flow, birds fly, trees blossom—but he himself is beyond change.

昭和辛卯夏
宜古郎
画並到替

入鄽
垂手

十

IN THE WORLD

The boy returns to the
world as a free man who
has transcended duality.
He does everything with
the whole of himself,
because he has nothing to
gain or lose. He manifests
the bodhisattva ideal
and forgoes liberation to
help others.

CHAPTER FIVE

PLUCKING THE FLOWER

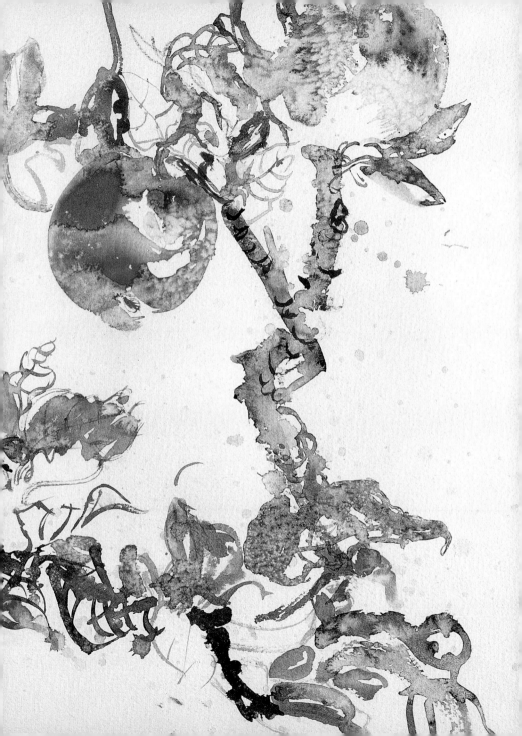

PLUCKING THE FLOWER

Taking monastic or priestly vows is one way to embark in the Zen life, but Zen has also attracted millions of lay followers worldwide.

There are many ways into Zen life. Since the Edo period (1600–1867 C.E.), the neighborhood Buddhist temple has been a cross between the local parish church, registry office, and cemetery. The position of temple priest has been hereditary for centuries, as only ordained monks and nuns were expected to be celibate. The other formal route is to become a candidate for ordination as a monk or nun in a Zen monastery. Although most monasteries are in Japan and Korea, there are a growing number of monastic establishments in North America and Europe.

The rituals surrounding the entrance of a candidate into a Zen monastery are steeped in the Japanese cultural tradition. The first thing he or she does is to take a hot bath—a daily occurrence in Japan where showers are still a relative novelty. The abbot then shaves the candidate's head, leaving a single lock of hair. The candidate, dressed in white as a symbol of purity, is presented to the community, or *sangha*. After he bows to the abbot and his or her parents, signifying a breaking of family attachments and admission into the sangha, the abbot shaves off the last remaining lock of hair. He then hands the candidate a black robe (*koromo*), signifying emptiness. After more prayers, the abbot gives the candidate a new name.

Life in the monastery is strictly timetabled, with daily periods set aside for sitting meditation, interviews with a teacher, and manual work. Buddhist monks and nuns are also expected to go into the outside world to beg for food, though this is largely symbolic and not a means of gaining subsistence.

In the Mahayana tradition, enlightenment is not reserved for ordained monks and nuns as in the Hinayana tradition. Millions of lay followers of Zen take part in retreats, meditate, and study in the same way as ordained brethren.

> Life in a Japanese monastery adheres to a strict routine of meditation, study, and work.

POINTERS OF
THE WAY

Because Zen is transmitted directly from mind to mind,
the teacher-pupil relationship plays a crucial role.

As can be expected from Zen, the role of the teacher, or roshi (old master), is a paradoxical one. After all, if we are all born with Buddha-nature, we have nothing to learn and they have nothing to teach. The relationship, however, is central to Zen practice because of the concept of direct transmission. The student and roshi develop an extremely close relationship, which can be compared to the one between patient and analyst in the West.

Even though he has nothing to teach, the roshi will unblock and uncover, point out any errors or divergences from Zen life, and attest to the student's understanding once he or she has experienced kensho, the initial enlightenment. The roshi, finally, is the only one qualified to award the student his or her inka-shomei, or certificate of enlightenment.

The teaching styles of the Rinzai-shu and Soto-shu are radically different. In Rinzai-shu Zen, the teacher is a dynamic, sometimes violent guide, who is suited to a teaching style that includes koans, shouts, and blows. The contrasting Soto-shu Zen style is no less strict or arduous, but far gentler, befitting a training system that consists mainly of zazen.

TRAINING TO BECOME A ROSHI

To complete the full roshi training in a Japanese Rinzai-shu Zen monastery, working through the five koan ranks, and other formalities, can take about 30 years. However, as we have seen from the lives of many of the great Ch'an, Son, and Zen masters, specially gifted or insightful individuals have attained enlightenment in a much shorter period of time. With very few exceptions, their satori was always attested to by a Zen master, who himself was in the Dharma line that stretched back through the centuries to the Buddha himself. Therefore the prospective student should be cautious about anyone who claims the title of Zen teacher, if he or she has not received an inka-shomei from a recognized roshi.

In the formal setting of a Japanese monastery, students go to see their roshi for regular *sanzen* (going to Zen) sessions. In Rinzai-shu Zen, private roshi-student meetings are called *dokusan*. These consist of question-and-answer exchanges, called *mondo* or *hossen* (Dharma contests). Mondo between ancient masters have become koans, which the roshi will then set for his students.

The roshi is indispensable in the student's path to enlightenment, and, once achieved, is the only one who can grant the inka-shomei.

"THE DHARMA GATE OF
GREAT REST AND JOY"

Although technically extremely simple, zazen sitting is very demanding, both mentally and physically.

Zazen (sitting meditation) is so central to Zen practice that the two are often thought to be one and the same. In Soto-shu Zen, it forms the bulk of training, and zazen itself is equated with satori, or enlightenment. Dogen, the founder of Soto-shu, gives detailed instructions for the correct performance of zazen—after describing the sitting position (see box), he goes on: "Now that your posture is in order, regulate your breathing. If a thought arises, take note of it and dismiss it. If you practice in this way for a long time, you will forget all attachments and concentration will come naturally. That is the art of zazen. Zazen is the Dharma gate of great rest and joy."

The zazen technique itself is extremely simple, and requires no rituals or complicated *mantra* (words or phrases which are chanted as objects of meditation). Beginners should concentrate on their breathing, counting cycles of ten breaths for the duration of a period of 40 or 50 minutes. A slightly more advanced practice is to follow the breaths without counting them. Finally, the most difficult form of zazen taught by Dogen is *shikantaza* (nothing but simply sitting), which does not employ any focus such as the breath. In Soto-shu zendo, sitters face a plain wall (mempeki) in commemoration of Bodhidharma's nine-year meditation facing a cave wall.

In the lotus position, the body is perfectly supported for the act of meditation.

HOW TO PRACTICE ZAZEN

The traditional postures for zazen are the yoga lotus (*padmasana*), half-lotus (*ardha-padmasana*), and correct seat (*seiza*), kneeling back on your heels. Your head and spine are held upright; your hands are in your lap with the back of your left hand resting on your right palm, thumbs together. Your eyes stay open. Your attention follows the breath, but your mind is centered in the *hara*, the energy center of the body, located just below your navel. All three postures are difficult for Westerners who are not accustomed to floor-level living. If you are going to attempt a cross-legged posture, place a rolled-up mat or cushion under your seat to help you maintain an upright spine. To make seiza more comfortable, kneel on a large cushion and place a smaller cushion under your seat to relieve the pressure on your leg joints. An alternative posture is to sit forward on a stool or a wooden chair.

Legend has it that Bodhidharma meditated for nine years in a cave.

THE
GATELESS GATE

The koan is not a verbal puzzle to be solved—
it is an obstacle that the student has to overcome.

Hakuin's famous question, "What is the sound of one hand clapping?", which opens this book, is a koan (public announcement). Koans take the form of questions, phrases, or single words that are given to a student of Zen by his teacher. Koans often contain paradoxical statements or puzzles, but the intention is not to test a student's lateral thinking. There is no clever answer to a koan, and for many students, there may be no answer at all.

THE SOUND OF
ONE HAND CLAPPING

Master Mokurai had a young novice in his charge named Toyo who was 12 years old. Toyo saw the older students visit Mokurai for sanzen and he, too, wished to receive training. His master told him he was too young, but the boy was so insistent that Mokurai finally asked him, "What is the sound of one hand clapping?"

Toyo went back to his room and, through the window, heard a geisha playing the *shamisen* (a stringed instrument like a banjo). He went back to Mokurai and gave the music the geisha had played as the answer. Mokurai quickly reprimanded him. "No, no," he said. "That will never do."

Toyo went back to his room and considered and rejected one sound after another: the sound of dripping water, the wind, the cry of an owl. All the sounds he could come up with, Mokurai turned down.

Finally, Toyo entered true meditation and transcended all sounds. "I could collect no more sounds," he told Mokurai. "So I reached the soundless sound." He had heard the sound of one hand clapping.

Students will meditate on koans during zazen, or they may carry them with them during their daily activities. The koan focuses the student's thoughts and stops his or her mind from wandering. The koan is like the grain of dust that irritates the oyster and makes it create a pearl. It is meant to break down the student's reliance on knowledge and logical thought. Beyond logic, it will also defy all metaphorical associations until, exhausted, the student grasps the response that will show his teacher that he or she has realized the truth the koan is designed to teach.

Monks will often carry koans with them—figuratively and literally—both in and out of the monastery.

Koans were first used to train students by the Lin-chi school of Ch'an Buddhism (Japanese: *Rinzai-shu*). Their first recorded use dates back to the ninth century C.E. One of the earliest koan collections is *The Blue Cliff Record* (Japanese: *Hekiganroku*), compiled by Yuan-wu K'o-ch'in (1036–1135, C.E.).

Probably the most famous Chinese collection is *The Gateless Gate* (Japanese: *Mumonkan*) by Wu-men Hui-k'ai (1183–1260 C.E.). In the introduction to the text, Wu-men explains how it came to be written:

A WATER BUFFALO PASSES THROUGH THE ENCLOSURE

Master Goso Hoen Zenji said, "It is like when a water buffalo leaves the safety of its enclosure to the edge of a cliff over an abyss. His horns, head, and hoofs pass through, but why can't his tail?"

Wu-men commented, "If anyone can open one eye at this point and utter a single word of Zen, he is qualified to repay the four gratifications and save the numberless sentient beings. But if he cannot utter a word of Zen at this time, he should turn back to his tail."

He then added the verse:
"If the buffalo runs, he will fall
    into the abyss;
If he returns, he will
    be butchered.
That little tail
Is a very strange thing."

"In the year 1228, the monks of Lung-hsiang monastery asked me for instruction. In my lectures, I retold the koans of old to inspire their practice. I meant to use the koans of the masters as a man might use a staff or stone to knock on a gate and, which, when the gate is opened, he throws away. When my notes were assembled, however, I was surprised to find that there were 48 koans, each with a commentary and verse. Although they were not given in any particular order, I have called the collection *The Gateless Gate* for students to read as a guide."

The first koan in the collection is informally known as *Joshu's Dog* which is given often to beginners as their first koan:

A monk asked Joshu, "Does a dog have Buddha-nature?"

Joshu exclaimed, "Mu!" (*Mu* in Chinese means "nothing" or "no".)

Wu-men added a prose commentary and a verse:

Has a dog got Buddha-nature?

This is the most serious question of all.

If you say yes or no, you lose your own Buddha-nature.

This is the barrier of Zen. If you pass through it, you will see Joshu face-to-face. Then you can work hand in hand with the whole line of patriarchs...If you want to pass this barrier, you must work through every bone of your body, through every pore of your skin, filled with this question: What is Mu? And carry it day and night. Do not believe that it is the common negative meaning nothing. It is not nothingness, the opposite of existence. If you really want to pass this barrier, you should feel like drinking a hot iron ball that you can neither swallow nor spit out."

Koans make up the bulk of training in *kanna Zen*, which is practiced by the Rinzai-shu. The Soto-shu also uses koans, but far more sparingly. Koans are set by the roshi to prevent "mind-wandering,"

Many Zen students will focus upon koans not only during meditation but also during their daily tasks.

and to act as a focus during zazen, but students also work on them during their daily tasks. Ultimately, they will trigger kensho, first enlightenment, and further satori experiences.

For hundreds of years, koans were part of Zen training, but their use was only formalized in the eighteenth century by the Rinzai-shu master and reformer, Hakuin Ekaku (1685–1768 C.E.) and his successors. They devised a method of teaching with koans, and divided them into the following five categories:

Hosshin koan (ultimate reality): These are intended to create an awareness of ultimate reality, or Buddha-nature. Working through these, the student may experience kensho.

Kikan koan (support): Although Buddha-nature is undifferentiated, these aim at giving the student the ability to discern distinction within non-distinction.

Gonsen koan (considering words): These consist of the difficult sayings of the patriarchs, and create an awareness of their deep meaning.

Nanto koan (difficult): These are the most difficult koans to pass through. The *Water Buffalo* is one of the nanto koan series.

Goi koan (five ranks): The final series of koan, when the other four have been worked out, these test and deepen individual insight.

KOAN STUDIES

Koans are provocative in that they encourage the student to interpret or explain material that is often presented as paradox or nonsense. It is only when the student has admitted that rational ways of thinking are fruitless that the koan will start to have true impact. Koans have often been described as hot coals in the soul—that is to say, they are not intended to be analyzed or digested. Instead, the student should repeatedly bring the essence of the koan to his or her awareness and wait for its meaning to make itself apparent spontaneously. In this way, some Zen masters have seen life itself as an extended koan, one which begs us to live in the moment and embrace spontaneity.

THE MAN IS
THE TEMPLE

Zen in Japan has inherited great buildings from its past, but the real temple of Zen is man himself.

The first thing that strikes the visitor to a major Japanese Zen temple complex, such as Daitokuji in Kyoto, is the extreme formality of its architecture. Zen temples are modeled on the Ch'an temples of Sung-dynasty China (960–1279 C.E.) with the various Buddha and study halls set on a North-South axis. The elements that give them a Chinese look are tiled floors, ogee windows, and slender pillars. Although the halls contain images of the Buddha and various bodhisattvas, these are not worshipped, nor are they the center of elaborate rituals as in other Buddhist schools.

The following story presents the Zen attitude to temples, relics, and statuary:

When the monk Tan-hsia (739–824 C.E.) was traveling, he stopped one night at a Ch'an temple. It was mid-winter and bitterly cold. Finding no fuel for the brazier, Tan-hsia burned the statue of the Buddha from the shrine. When the temple priest scolded him the next day, Tan-hsia replied, "I was trying to get the Buddha's bones and ashes (the most precious Buddhist relics)."

"How can you get the Buddha's bones and ashes from a piece of wood?" the priest asked.

"If it is no more than a piece of wood, why do you scold me?" was Tan-hsia's reply.

The real business of Zen teaching in Daitokuji does not take place in formal halls, which are shut most of the time, but in its many sub-temples, hidden behind walls, and hedges. Within these enclosures are smaller, less formal buildings. Built in the traditional *shoin* style, these single-story temples have *tatami* mat floors, and broad, wooden verandas overlooking carefully laid out gardens. Sub-temples, such as Daitokuji's Koto-in, do not look like religious buildings, and are only temples by virtue of being the residence of monks. In Zen, man himself is the temple.

> Many Zen temples contain fabulous images of bodhisattvas and of the Buddha, but these are not themselves objects of worship.

COLLECTING
HEART AND MIND

*Life in a monastery or retreat is lived according to a strict
and demanding timetable of meditation and work.*

Both laymen and ordained monks and nuns attend formal sessions of zazen in a meditation hall, or zendo. In a Japanese zendo, the image of the Buddha is on the back wall, with the cushions on which the monks sit laid out along the walls. In Soto-shu practice, the students face the wall (mempeki). The layout of Chinese and Korean halls is slightly different. In China, the Buddha image is in the center of the room, whereas in Korea, the monks sit in two lines in the middle of the room. The officiating monk begins the session with an invocation, by striking a gong or wooden clapper.

Students in a zendo meditate with their eyes open.

The sitters meditate in complete silence for 40 or 50 minutes. At a signal from the officiating monk, the sitters stand up for 10 minutes of walking meditation (Japanese: *kinhin*). The Japanese is the most formal style of kinhin, with the monks going around the hall clockwise, holding their hands at chest height.

A monitor patrols the room during zazen, carrying the kyosaku (or *keisaku*, wake-up stick). He will deliver two lightning strikes to the shoulders of any sitter seen to be slouching or dozing. A sitter can also request a blow from the kyosaku, which will help with his or her concentration. The kyosaku itself represents the sword of the bodhisattva Manjushri that cuts through all delusions.

In a Zen monastery, one week in every month is set aside for an intensive period of zazen. This is known as *sesshin* (collecting heart and mind). The time allocated to zazen increases to nine or ten hours a day, taking precedence over all other activities. Meals are taken in the zendo, and the abbot or roshi will deliver a daily lecture, or *keisho*. Zen retreats in the West usually last for one week and follow the daily timetable of sesshin.

SESSHIN

4:00 A.M.	Wake up
4:30 A.M.	Zazen and kinhin
6:30 A.M.	Chanting
7:00 A.M.	Morning meal
7:30 A.M.	Cleaning
8:00-11:30 A.M.	Zazen and kinhin
11:30 A.M.	Chanting
11:45 A.M.	Noon meal
1:00 P.M.	Rest
2:00 P.M.	Zazen
2:30 P.M.	Lecture
3:30–6:00 P.M.	Zazen and kinhin
6:00 P.M.	Evening meal
6:45–7:30 P.M.	Rest
7:30–9:00 P.M.	Zazen and kinhin
9:30 P.M.	Sleep

FROM THE
INSIDE OUT

Zen is not a religion of external trappings; as a lay student, you do not have to learn a foreign tongue or shave your head.

How can Zen—a philosophy with its origins in sixth-century India—have any relevance to the life of the twenty-first-century Westerner? Despite its great antiquity, Zen is surprisingly modern. Although it is grounded in a framework of Japanese ritual, etiquette, and scholarship, this is secondary, not fundamental to living the Zen life. You do not have to know the meaning of the Japanese word zazen to sit in meditation, or the word kensho to experience enlightenment. Zen has no beliefs—even the Ten Grave Precepts are only guidelines. If you encounter a strong belief, be it in the Buddha himself, during zazen, you are instructed to disregard it totally, because even belief, which is part of

Zen is a way of life that can be followed by anyone and attracts lay students both in the East and the West.

the ego, will prevent the realization of one's egoless Buddha-nature.

Zen is not one of those Eastern religions that asks you to transform yourself from the outside in. You do not have to change your clothes, shave your head, or learn a foreign language; at most, you might need to invest in a couple of cushions. Zen, of course, will transform your life, but it will do it from the inside out. The insight you acquire through meditation and study will change the way you think and, by degrees, will transform the way you live, work, and conduct your relationships.

"ORDINARY MIND"

Joshu asked his master, Nansen, "What is the way?"

"Ordinary mind is the way," replied Nansen.

"How do I find the ordinary mind?" asked Joshu.

"If you look for it, you will lose it," said Nansen. "The way is not a matter of knowing or not knowing. Knowing is delusion, not knowing is confusion. When you have found the true way, you will find that it is vast and without end."

ZEN MIND, BEGINNER'S MIND

Two outstanding Japanese teachers brought Zen to the United States during the twentieth century.

The first Zen master to visit the United States was Soyen Shaku, who attended the World Parliament of Religions, held in Chicago in 1893. One of his students, the scholar Daisetsu Taitaro Suzuki (1870–1966 C.E.), was offered a job with a religious publisher in Chicago in 1897. Accepting the post, he determined to experience satori before leaving for his new life in the United States. He redoubled his efforts and, after ten months of intensive study, was finally enlightened. He was the first Japanese to write on Zen in English from his first-hand experience. His three-volume *Essays in Zen Buddhism* began to appear

in 1927. He stayed in the United States for 13 years, returning to Japan in 1909 to teach English. In 1922, he was appointed professor of Buddhist philosophy at Otani University in Kyoto.

The second and, without doubt, the most significant figure in the transmission of Soto-shu Zen to the United States was another Suzuki (though no relation of D.T. Suzuki), Shunryu Suzuki (1905–71 C.E.). During the Pacific War (1941–45) between

This painting shows a traveling monk, wearing a hat, and holding a fan. He has a heavy load of sutras on his back.

Japan and the United States, he organized a pacifist group, which must have been extremely difficult in the militaristic climate of wartime Japan.

Shunryu Suzuki was a key figure in introducing Zen to the United States.

In 1958, he was invited to San Francisco to take charge of the local Soto-shu chapter. Initially, he had thought to stay a year or two before returning to Japan, but was so charmed by the United States and its people that he decided to stay there and teach. Setting up the San Francisco Zen Center, he soon had a group of 60 students around him. Next, he founded the first Zen monastery outside of Asia at Tassajara Springs in California. His talks were collated and published in 1970 as *Zen Mind, Beginner's Mind*. For Suzuki, the beginner's mind, ever open to new experiences, is close to the original mind or Buddha-nature.

EAST MEETS WEST

The twentieth century witnessed the transmission of Buddhist traditions to the West, notably Tibetan Buddhism and Zen.

Buddhism was introduced to the West at the end of the nineteenth century, soon after Japan reopened its doors to the outside world after two-and-a-half centuries of isolation. Although Zen interested philosophers and intellectuals, it made little headway with the overwhelmingly Christian population until the postwar period.

Increased contacts between Japan and the West post-1945 meant that an ever-growing number of Europeans and North Americans were exposed to Zen teachings. Zen became fashionable among writers and artists, notably the Beat Generation poets and writers, (such as Alan Ginsberg) as well as psychoanalysts and psychotherapists. One major figure influenced by its

Korean monasteries, such as this one, have become the model for many Western establishments.

teachings was Fritz Perls (1893–1970 C.E.), the creator of Gestalt therapy. Zen is now firmly established in the West, with its own teachers, temples, and monasteries, which cater to a growing number of students.

In the West, Zen has become associated with a basic, minimalist approach to interior design.

New waves of immigrants from Korea and Vietnam in the postwar period have brought with them different traditions of Zen teaching. A leading exponent of Korean Son in the United States is Seung Sahn (also known as Soen-sa, b.1927 C.E.), who has tried to blend traditional Oriental teaching methods with the Californian lifestyle. Zen now has a thriving European and North American sangha, which is producing full-fledged Zen roshi, including the influential author of *Three Pillars of Zen*, Philip Kapleau.

Running in tandem with the formal transmission of Zen, there has also been another non-religious transmission of Zen to Europe and North America. This has been through the dissemination of Japan's traditional arts and martial arts, and the development of a Zen "lifestyle," which tries to apply Zen principles to interior design, cookery, and gardening.

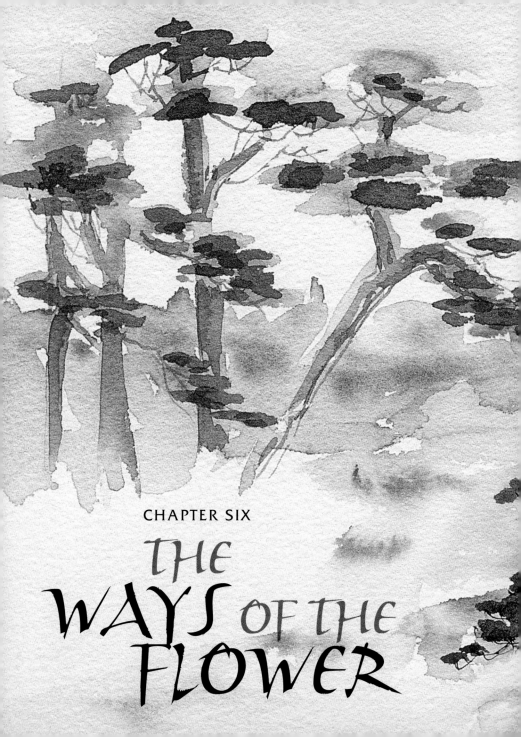

CHAPTER SIX

THE
WAYS OF THE
FLOWER

THE WAYS OF THE FLOWER

The traditional arts or "ways" of Japan are seen as another way to practice the teachings of Zen Buddhism.

Zen has been instrumental in shaping Japan's traditional arts, or "ways"—ink painting, calligraphy, the tea ceremony, poetry, martial arts, and flower arrangement—as well as its architecture, interior, and garden design.

The Zen "ways" are seen as alternative means of realizing enlightenment. To excel in any of the traditional arts, the practitioner must go beyond mere technical proficiency; his or her creative actions have to be completely spontaneous, and free from intention and selfishness. Many of Japan's great Zen masters, such as Hakuin, Ikkyu, and Ryokan, are also recognized to be among its greatest poets, painters, and calligraphers. Conversely, artists such as the poet Matsuo Basho, and the tea master Sen no Rikyu, are seen as having a deep understanding of Zen.

The paired concepts of *wabi* and *sabi* are at the very heart of the Zen aesthetic. Notoriously difficult to translate into English, the meanings of these words overlap. Wabi (from the Japanese verb, *wabu*, "to languish," and the adjective, *wabishi*, "lonely and without comfort") is an aesthetic and moral principle that advocates living a quiet, leisurely life, free from worldly concerns. Its spiritual dimension is an implied liberation from all material and emotional attachments. Sabi, fostered by the poet Matsuo Basho and his followers, has associations with old age, desolation, and loneliness. Again, while these feelings might suggest negative connotations, they are viewed in a positive light from the perspective of someone who has transcended transient worldly attachments for a far greater prize.

Zen "style" has become a cliché of Western design. Where its advocates have retained the simplicity of line, stripped of all ornament, and the functionalism of Zen, creating the minimalist style, they have lost sight of the rich spiritual dimension that is the true foundation of the Zen "ways."

The Zen spirit displays itself in both peaceful and martial art forms.

THE ABODE OF
VACANCY

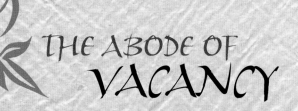

The ultimate expression of the Zen aesthetic of wabi-sabi is the Japanese tea ceremony.

The ceremonial drinking of tea began in China in ancient times. During the T'ang dynasty (618–907 C.E.), tea was boiled with salt and butter, as it still is today in Tibet. Tea was first drunk in Japan during the Heian period (794–1185 C.E.), but it remained an aristocratic pastime until its cultivation was popularized by the founder of the Rinzai-shu, Eisai, who recommended its use on health grounds. Zen monks drank tea from a communal bowl, as a form of communion celebrating their fellowship, and also to help them to stay awake during meditation.

The two tea masters who created the tea ceremony, or chanoyu (tea's hot water), which is still practiced in Japan, were Takeno Joo (1502–55 C.E) and his disciple, Sen no Rikyu (1522–1591 C.E). Turning his back on the elaborate and luxurious tea ceremonies of earlier periods, Sen no Rikyu

TEA

The tea ceremony had its origins in worship of Bodhidharma, who is said to have pulled off his eyebrows to prevent himself from falling asleep while meditating. Legend has it that tea plants sprung up where his eyelids fell to the earth. Although the tea ceremony today is highly ritualistic, the purpose remains the unification of body and mind. The ceremony may appear over-meticulous and stylized, but in fact preserves the utmost simplicity of movement.

This 17th-century woodblock print shows a Japanese tea seller, who would have been a central figure in the society of the day.

created a ritual steeped in the philosophy and aesthetics of Zen. His *wabicha* (poverty tea) was a form of meditation that was meant to relieve the mind from its daily stresses and bring inner peace. He specified that the ceremony be held in a purpose-built teahouse modeled on a rustic hermitage.

The four guests at the ceremony first wash their hands in a stone basin to purify themselves. They have to stoop to enter the teahouse through a low door, symbolic of their humility and equal status. The inside is as plain and unfinished as the outside, the only decoration being a single, carefully selected scroll and a flower arrangement in the alcove, or *tokonoma*. The equipment, such as the metal kettle and tea bowls, although extremely valuable, look simple and unadorned. Even though the etiquette of the tea ceremony is complex, its aim is spontaneity and ease between the host and his guests. The tea ceremony and its related arts were first introduced in the West by Okakura Kakuzo in the *Book of Tea*, which was first published in New York in 1906.

HEAVEN, MAN, AND EARTH

Another of Japan's ancient traditional arts to be influenced by Zen is the Way of Flowers, *or flower arrangement.*

The art of *ikebana*, "living flowers," also known as *kado* (way of flowers), began as offerings for Buddhist altars. The first school of ikebana, the Ikenobo school, was founded by the seventh-century nobleman-turned-Buddhist-monk, Senmu. A traditional arrangement explores the relationship between man and nature in a transient world. A tall stem represents heaven, a medium length one, humanity, and a short one, the earth. Arrangements are asymmetrical, using odd numbers, such as three, five, and seven. Space is incorporated as a design element, as is the Taoist yin-yang principle of balancing opposites. Following the wabi-sabi ideals, the arrangement is understated, depending on simplicity of line, rather than color, to make it impactful.

A related tradition of Zen-inspired *kado*, Sen no Rikyu's *chabana* "tea flowers," are meant to look completely natural and unarranged. Tea flower arrangements often use a single flower in a bamboo or ceramic container placed in the alcove, or tokonoma, directly beneath a ink-wash painting or calligraphy, or hung on one of the wooden uprights that frame the alcove.

In the *Book of Tea*, Okakura relates the story of Sen no Rikyu's peony to illustrate the ideals of chabana. Sen no Rikyu served the Taiko, or military ruler of Japan, Toyotomi Hideyoshi (1537–1598 C.E.). One day, the Taiko saw a bed of the most beautiful peonies in the garden of Rikyu's house. Complimenting Rikyu on the flowers, he said he would return the next day to view them at his leisure. When the Taiko returned the following day, every single peony had been uprooted. Furious, he stormed into the tearoom to upbraid Rikyu, when he saw, in a container the single most beautiful of the peonies from the garden, masterfully displayed, and appearing as if it had been picked a moment before.

Zen flower arrangements symbolize the relationship between man, earth, and heaven.

Zen landscapes are reproduced using stones, white sand, and sparse plantings.

The twelfth through sixteenth centuries saw the heyday of the Zen garden. Known as "dry stone gardens," or *karesansui*, they used an extremely limited palette of elements: natural rocks, mosses, trees, and of coarse, white sand. The aim of these gardens was to give the viewer an intimation of the hidden oneness that underlies the multiplicity of appearance. The landscape is used in a purely symbolic fashion, like a three-dimensional version of an ink-wash painting.

Perhaps the most famous dry stone garden is the one created by Soami (1472–1525 C.E.) at Ryoanji in Kyoto in 1513. A rough brown wall frames the large, rectangular garden. It contains three groupings of 15 rocks amid swirls of meticulously raked white sand. The exact meaning and symbolism of the rocks has been a subject of debate for several centuries. They have been variously defined as islands within the ocean, a stylized Chinese character, or a mother tiger and her cubs.

An example of a walk-through Zen garden is the *chaniwa* (tea garden), which embodies the ideals of simplicity and rusticity in a framework of understated natural beauty. The winding path that leads from the gateway to the teahouse is the compressed version of a path that would take the guests from the bustle of the city to the tranquillity of a mountain hermitage.

"YOU *PAINT* THE BRANCH WELL, AND YOU HEAR THE *WIND*"

Zen painting does not seek to faithfully reproduce reality but to capture its momentary essence.

Many Ch'an and Zen masters have excelled in the closely related arts of ink-wash painting (*sumi-e*) and calligraphy (*shodo*, way of the brush). Both these arts make use of the same materials: bamboo and natural bristle brushes, inksticks that have to be ground on an inkstone and the ink diluted to the right consistency with water, and fragile, absorbent *washi* (handmade paper). The aim of both ink-wash painting and calligraphy is to capture the immediacy and spontaneity of the moment of creation by transmitting one's spiritual energy into the work. The touch must be light, fluid, and continuous.

In ink-wash painting, unlike Western oil painting or watercolor, neither preliminary sketch nor correction is possible once the brushstroke has been made. There are no rules of composition, symmetry, or perspective, and the emphasis is on dynamism rather than accuracy or fidelity to nature.

The concept of *li* (principle) is at the heart of Ch'an ink-wash painting. To properly represent the li of his subject, the painter must abandon the ego that would intrude between the brush and the subject. While the natural world is the most common subject, ink-wash painting also has a strong tradition of depicting human subjects. Rather than formal portraits, the Zen and Ch'an representations of the patriarchs are irreverent caricatures, showing them in undignified postures. A favorite subject is the pot-bellied Chinese god of good fortune, Pu-tei (Japanese: *Hotei*), who represents the joyful spontaneous experience of the Zen life.

In contrast to Western monastic calligraphy, with its slow laborious copying and elaborate use of ornament, color, and gold leaf, East Asian calligraphy is spontaneous and immediate. The master interprets the chosen Chinese character (Japanese: *kanji*) on the empty white ground in a single movement. Again, there is no sketch or correction. Favored subjects in Zen calligraphy are the character *ichi*, the number one, signifying the unitary nature of reality, and the circle, representing emptiness.

> While landscapes are popular themes, portraiture, flora, and trees are also common in Zen painting.

"A FROG JUMPS IN"

The literary embodiment of the Zen aesthetic is to be found in the work of the haiku master, Matsuo Basho.

The *haiku* (or *hokku*) is a Japanese verse form consisting of three lines of 5–7–5 syllables. Traditionally, it contains a reference to the season during which it was written. In contrast to the elevated courtly *waka* poetry, the haiku was originally the opening triplet of a linked verse form known as the *haikai*. Until the seventeenth century C.E., the haikai was little more than a literary game in which the players displayed their literary knowledge and wit. It was only when Matsuo Basho and his followers took up the haiku that it acquired its Zen associations. Under Basho's brush, it became the perfect expression of the poet's experience of Buddha-nature.

The Zen spirit may be expressed artistically through painting or poetry.

There are several stories relating how Basho came to write his most famous haiku about a frog jumping into a pond. Basho was a devoted follower of Buddhism, who studied and understood the most difficult of the *sutras*. According to legend, he went to visit the Zen master Takuan. They sat on the veranda overlooking the temple garden, the centerpiece of which was a large ornamental pond. They talked for many hours and Basho gave learned answers to Takuan's questions.

At last Takuan said, "You are a devoted believer and a great man, but in all the time we have spoken, I have only heard you quote the words of the Buddha or of eminent teachers. I would like to hear your own words. Quickly give me a sentence of your own."

For the first time Basho was perplexed and could not reply. His mind was a complete blank, and he seemed incapable of moving or speaking.

"I thought you understood Buddhism," Takuan continued. "Why can't you answer me?"

At that moment, there was a noise in the garden. Basho instantly said:

An ancient pond
A frog jumps in
"Splash!"

Takuan laughed and exclaimed, "These are the words of your true self!"

BASHO'S POETRY

The scope and variety of Basho's haiku output are enormous: a selection of his poems are presented beneath.

Breakfast enjoyed
in the fine company of
morning glories

A solitary
crow on a bare branch
autumn evening

Nothing in the cry
of cicadas suggests they
are about to die

Awakened at midnight
by the sound of the water jar
cracking from the ice

Though thin and weak
the chrysanthemum
inevitably will bud

Along this way
no travellers
dusk in autumn

THE WAYS OF THE WARRIOR

*The samurai ideal of bushido has become the
"spirit" of the modern Japanese martial arts.*

During the height of the power of the samurai, between the twelfth and sixteenth centuries C.E., Zen was seen as an integral part of bushido, the "Way of the Warrior." The two weapons' techniques (Japanese: *jutsu*), favored by the Japanese warrior were swordplay (*kenjutsu*) and archery (*kyujutsu*). To become a truly great swordsman, the warrior had to first transcend his fear of injury and death. Like the master painter or calligrapher, the samurai's moves not only had to be technically perfect, but also totally spontaneous and free from intention. One second of hesitation might mean the difference between life and death during an encounter.

After the introduction of firearms in the sixteenth century, the usefulness of these skills on the battlefield diminished. The samurai, however, continued to train in the use of the sword and bow, although the aim of the training was increasingly spiritual rather than practical. What had formerly been techniques, now became "ways." Kenjutsu became *kendo* (way of the sword), which used a bamboo sword, and kyujtsu became *kyudo* (way of the bow). Although these could still be used for self-defense, their function was self-knowledge, and the life-and-death struggle was no longer with an adversary, but with one's own ego.

While in kendo, now a sport in modern Japan, the element of competition still remains, in kyudo, hitting the target is secondary to the ritual of loosing the arrow. Archers develop an inner balance of mind and an outer control of the body, and the ideal is to fire in a state of non-thought (Japanese: *mushin*). For the kyudo master, the target and arrow have become one, and there can be no feeling of accomplishment or failure, of good or bad.

These ideals have been transmitted to the more modern martial arts of *karatedo* (way of the empty hand), *judo* (way of suppleness), and *aikido* (way of harmony), all three of which are unarmed fighting systems that were created at the turn of the twentieth century.

> Zen is very closely associated with Japanese archery and fencing.

GLOSSARY

Bodhisattva:
"Enlightenment-being," a being who has taken the vow to save all sentient beings, and the highest state of the disciple of the Mahayana tradition of Buddhism.

Buddha-nature:
(Budhata, Bussho). The undifferentiated nature underlying the world of phenomenal appearances. In Mahayana Buddhism, all humans are born with Buddha-nature and are equally able to become bodhisattvas.

Bushido:
"Way of the warrior," the set of moral precepts and ideals that governed the conduct of the samurai warrior during Japan's feudal period.

Ch'an:
"Meditation, absorption," Chinese translation of the Sanskrit Dhyana, Korean Son, and Japanese Zen.

Chanoyu:
"Tea's hot water," also chado ("the way of tea"). The tea ceremony formulated by the tea master Sen no Rikyu, which combines wabi-sabi aesthetics with Zen spirituality.

Dharma:
"Uphold," the teachings of the historical Buddha, including the Four Noble Truths and the Eightfold Noble Path.

Dhyana:
(also Jhana) meditation. The school of Indian Buddhism brought to China by Bodhidharma. It gave rise to Ch'an in China, Son in Korea, and Zen in Japan.

Haiku:
Japanese verse form consisting of three lines of 5–7–5 syllables. Taking its themes from nature, the haiku is the literary expression of the wabi-sabi ideal.

Hinayana:
The "Lesser Vehicle," one of the two main Buddhist traditions, which believes that there only can be one Buddha per historical cycle and that the highest state a disciple can attain is that of arhat.

"Ho!":
(Japanese: "Kwatz!") Shout used in Rinzai-shu Zen training to shock a student into enlightenment. It is also used to symbolize the Dharma-succession between master and disciple.

Ikebana:
"Living flowers," also known as kado ("the way of flowers"), usually translated as the art of flower arrangement. Many schools of ikebana exist in Japan, most having close links with Buddhism.

Inka-shomei:
"Seal of recognition," confirming that someone is a Dharma-successor and allowed to call himself a roshi, or teacher.

Joriki:
A balancing of the mind during zazen that brings great elation and physical energy.

Karma:
The law of cause and effect that governs the world of appearances.

Kendo:
Traditional Japanese fencing using a bamboo sword.

Kensho:
"Seeing nature," the first experience of seeing Buddha-nature, which is a prelude of further experiences of satori.

Koan:
"Public announcement," a phrase or question used in Zen training to end a student's dependence on logical thought and test his understanding.

Kyosaku or Keisaku:
"Wake-up stick," a stick or staff used by Zen masters to shock pupils into enlightenment, and, during zazen, to awaken a dozing or daydreaming student.

Kyudo:
Traditional Japanese archery, using a plain, wooden bow.

Mahayana:
The "Great Vehicle," one of the two traditions of Buddhism popular in China, Korea, and Japan, for which the highest duty of the disciple is to work for the enlightenment of all sentient beings.

Mempeki:
"Facing the wall," sitting in zazen meditation, which is practiced in Soto Zen.

Mondo:
Question-and- answer session between master and pupil that is often recorded as koans.

Rinzai-shu:
(Chinese: Lin-chi), school of Japanese Zen Buddhism that advocates sudden enlightenment.

Roshi:
Teacher who has received his or her inka-shomei from a Zen master.

Sangha:
In Hinayana Buddhism, the community of ordained monks and nuns, but in Mahayana Buddhism, all adherents to Buddhism.

Sanzen:
Visiting a Zen master, or roshi, for instruction.

Satori:
Enlightenment, the ability to perceive the underlying principle of the world, Buddha-nature.

Sesshin:
Intensive period of zazen practice in a Japanese monastery.

Shakyamuni:
Name given to the historical Buddha, Siddharta Gautama.

Shikantaza:
A form of zazen sitting meditation advocated by Dogen, founder of the Soto-shu.

Shodo:
"Way of the brush," art of Japanese calligraphy.

Skandas:
The five conditions that make us human: form, sensation, mental activity, perception, and consciousness

Son:
Korean school of Dhyana Buddhism.

Soto-shu:
(Chinese: Ts'ao tung), school of Japanese Zen founded by Dogen.

Sumie:
"Ink-wash painting," painting technique using monochrome ink washes.

Sunyata:
Mahayana doctrine of the emptiness of form posited by the Indian philosopher Nagarjuna.

Sutra:
"Thread," collections of the teachings of the Buddha, and the later additions of the Mahayana tradition, which have been accorded canonical status, such as the *Lotus Sutra*.

Theravada:
"Teachings of the ancients," school of Sri Lankan and Southeast Asian Buddhism, and the only school of Hinayana Buddhism that has survived in the modern world.

Vajrayana:
Esoteric school of Buddhism found in Tibet and Mongolia, which bases its teachings on the *Tantras*.

Wabi-sabi:
Aesthetic concepts underlying all of Japan's traditional arts or "ways," usually translated as poverty, loneliness, old or faded things, and tranquility.

Zazen:
"Sitting meditation," the foundation of Zen practice.

Zendo:
Zen meditation hall.

INDEX

CREDITS

Quarto would like to thank and acknowledge the following for providing pictures reproduced in this book:

Ann Ronan Picture Library p13; Art Directors and TRIP/T Bognar p17; Art Directors and TRIP/Dinodia p12; Art Directors and TRIP/M Fairman p117; Art Directors and TRIP/F Good p18; Art Directors and TRIP/T Morse p49, p116, p123; Art Directors and TRIP/C Rennie p43; Art Directors and TRIP/A Tovy p19, p111; The British Museum p23, p70, p104, p120; Eli Charne/www.photobits.com p51; Catherine Karnow/CORBIS p115; Kimbell Art Museum/CORBIS p91; Chris Lisle/CORBIS p.45, p96; Su Chin Ee p8–9, p20–21, p37, p38, p40–41, p55, p60–61, p65, p77, p84–85, p108–109, p119; Don Farber p29, p87, p89, p95, p100; Gamma/Savolainen Sylvain p50; Heritage Images/British Library p11, p73; Heritage Images/British Museum p26, p30, p71, p113; Korean National Tourist Board p106; TopFoto.co.uk p27, p107

Quarto would like to extend grateful thanks to Su Chin Ee for her expert advice and guidance with the illustrations.

All other photographs and illustrations are the copyright of Quarto. While every effort has been made to credit contributors, we apologize should there have been any omissions or errors.